World History Matters

A Student Guide to World History Online

World History Matters

A Student Guide to World History Online

Kristin Lehner
The Johns Hopkins University

Kelly Schrum
George Mason University

T. Mills Kelly
George Mason University

Bedford/St. Martin's

Boston ◆ New York

For Bedford/St. Martin's
Publisher for History: Mary Dougherty
Director of Development for History: Jane Knetzger
Developmental Editor: Louise Townsend
Production Editor: Lindsay DiGianvittorio
Senior Production Supervisor: Dennis Conroy
Executive Marketing Manager: Jenna Bookin Barry
Editorial Assistant: Katherine Flynn
Copyeditor: Steven M. Patterson
Text Design: Lisa Buckley Design
Cover Design: Sara Gates
Composition: Achorn International
Printing and Binding: Haddon Craftsman, Inc., an RR Donnelley & Sons Company

President: Joan E. Feinberg
Editorial Director: Denise B. Wydra
Director of Marketing: Karen R. Soeltz
Director of Editing, Design, and Production: Marcia Cohen
Assistant Director of Editing, Design, and Production: Elise S. Kaiser
Managing Editor: Elizabeth M. Schaaf

Library of Congress Control Number: 2008932661

Manufactured in the United States of America.

3 2 1 0 9 8
f e d c b a

For information, write: Bedford/St. Martin's, 75 Arlington Street, Boston, MA 02116 (617-319-4000)

ISBN-10: 0–312–48582–4
ISBN-13: 978–0–312–48582–5

Dedication

We dedicate this book to Roy Rosenzweig (1950–2007), founder of the Center for History and New Media, leader and visionary in the field of digital humanities, and friend and mentor to so many.

Preface

In the twenty-first century, the Internet is ubiquitous, an integral part of our daily lives. We communicate, work, check news, traffic, and weather, and we play online. It is also a powerful tool for learning and researching history. Little more than a decade ago, the Web offered limited access to serious historical scholarship and primary source archives. A search on a figure of significant import to world history such as Mahatma Gandhi yielded a few of his writings with little context or fanfare. Today, however, a *Google* search on "Mahatma Gandhi" returns more than 5 million results, from a *Wikipedia* entry to sites with Gandhi's writings as well as photographs and audio and video clips of the Indian political and spiritual leader.

There are now hundreds of millions of primary sources available online for studying the past, as well as reliable and accessible secondary sources. The very abundance of the offerings, however, creates new challenges. Students and teachers continually ask: How do I find valuable materials? How can I quickly identify resources that will help me with a specific topic? How do I avoid misleading and even fraudulent documents? *World History Matters* provides a solution, offering a safe path through the overwhelming mass of historical sources and interpretations available online by providing an annotated guide to exemplary websites for the study of world history. The guide is selective, rather than comprehensive, highlighting 150 websites that present a compelling and broad range of resources for studying themes, topics, and regions throughout the global past. It emphasizes collections of primary sources with the goal of helping students learn to conduct historical research and to quickly locate reliable websites for doing so.

Content and Organization

World History Matters opens with a comprehensive introduction to history research online, emphasizing valuable resources, potential pitfalls (and how to avoid them), and guidance for working with online primary and secondary sources, from how to tell them apart to how to analyze them. The introduction presents strategies for navigating the Web as well as for helping students make the most of Web 2.0 resources, discussing the recent explosion of collaborative and participatory websites such as wikis and YouTube and their impact on historical research. Plagiarism is especially prevalent in the online era, and our section titled "A Word About Plagiarism" provides tips to help students understand and avoid it, followed by a guide to citing online resources.

The remainder of the volume is devoted to 150 carefully chosen and annotated history websites drawn from *World History Matters*, a website created and maintained by George Mason University's Center for History and New Media

(CHNM). With portals to the two sites *World History Sources* (**http://chnm.gmu.edu/worldhistorysources/**) and *Women in World History* (**http://chnm.gmu.edu/wwh/index.php**), this website offers hundreds of website reviews from which the 150 for this guide have been culled. The list begins with a section "General Websites for World History Research" that presents websites addressing themes throughout world history or across multiple time periods. The remaining annotations are arranged chronologically into broad time periods and cross-referenced to related websites that fit in another time period. The website annotations, drawn from the longer reviews on the *World History Matters* website, are relatively short by design. They provide a snapshot of the resources available on each website and a sense of its strengths and weaknesses. (We encourage you to visit the *World History Matters* websites for longer reviews and additional resources.) Specially designed icons allow students to quickly identify those websites that contain primary documents, images, and audio, video, map, and statistical resources. The book closes with a set of helpful appendices — a "Glossary of Common Internet Terms," an alphabetical list of the websites reviewed, and an index of topics, sources, and regions.

The Internet now offers an abundance of quality online materials unavailable even a decade ago and we hope this guide will prove a valuable resource to students in navigating many of these sites. It is important to remember that vast quantities of primary sources, such as diaries, films, and manuscript collections are not available digitally and may never be, and that secondary sources are often most easily available in print in the library. But given the riches available online, this book is intended as a guide to navigating them wisely and efficiently, as well as learning how to study the context and content of the sources and topics in question. The most important way to become an intelligent consumer of historical resources online is to become a good historian by learning to use and apply the skills of critical analysis that historians rely upon.

Note to Teachers: Teaching Resources Available on the *World History Matters* Websites

The two websites on which this guide is based, *World History Sources* and *Women in World History,* offer three valuable resources for teaching world history. The first is a set of website reviews with specific teaching ideas. For example, Michael Chang's review of the website *Hedda Morrison Photographs of China, 1933–1946* [110], at **http://chnm.gmu.edu/worldhistorysources/d/84/whm.html**, offers suggestions on how to use the images contained in this collection and how to juxtapose them with other online photographs of China. Similarly, Matthew Karush's review of *Mexico: From Empire to Revolution* [89], at **http://chnm.gmu.edu/worldhistorysources/d/45/whm.html**, contains useful ideas for creating manageable assignments from the vast collection of material available on this website. These are just two examples of the more than 200 website reviews you can explore to find valuable suggestions for teaching with online materials.

The second resource specifically designed for teachers is a set of twenty-five teaching case studies, located at **http://chnm.gmu.edu/wwh/casestudies.php** and http://chnm.gmu.edu/worldhistorysources/whmteaching.html. In these brief essays, experienced teachers describe how they used a primary source in a particular course. Each essay offers specific advice on preparation, classroom exercises, and assessment of student success. The essays also discuss how the activity could be improved. The case study by historian Thomas Ewing, for example, uses John Ledyard's journal account of his Pacific Ocean voyage from the 1770s to explore how Europeans described indigenous people of "other" worlds during the Age of Exploration.[1] Another case study on gender and race in colonial Latin America by historian Nora Jaffary uses eighteenth-century legal cases involving the contact between non-elite peoples with those of higher social status to examine the interplay of gender and racial ideologies in colonial Latin America.[2]

Finally, visit the *Women in World History* website (http://chnm.gmu.edu/wwh/modules.php) for a series of teaching modules that provide an introductory essay, annotated primary sources, and specific teaching tips and strategies. Topics range from Bhakti poets, originating in South of India in the sixth century C.E., to the Puerto Rican labor movement, Southeast Asian politics, and life under Stalinism in the twentieth century.

Visit the Center for History and New Media website (http://chnm.gmu.edu) to explore additional world history websites, such as *Liberty, Equality, Fraternity: Exploring the French Revolution*; *Children and Youth in History*; *Gulag: Many Days, Many Lives*; and *Making the History of 1989*.

Acknowledgments

This book is truly a collaborative effort. As noted above, it emerged from two websites, *World History Sources* and *Women in World History*, created by the Center for History and New Media (CHNM) at George Mason University, and brings together the expertise of world history scholars from around the globe. The group that developed *World History Sources* and *Women in World History* includes: Margarie Bingham, Rustin Crandall, Susan Gross, Katharina Hering, Stephanie Hurter, T. Mills Kelly, Kristin Lehner, Sharon Leon, Jessica May, Rikk Mulligan, Elena Razlogova, Mary Rojas, Roy Rosenzweig, Paula Petrik, Kelly Schrum, Amanda Shuman, and Peter Stearns. The 150 websites chosen specifically for *World History Matters* were selected and edited by editors Kristin Lehner and Kelly Schrum. The many scholars who authored the website reviews that are the basis for this book deserve special recognition as well: a list of their names and initials, affiliations, and academic specialties follows (note that these review authors' initials are included at the end of each annotation for which they are responsible).

[1] Thomas Ewing, "John Ledyard's Journal: Using Personal Narratives to Teach World History," *World History Sources*, http://chnm.gmu.edu/worldhistorysources/d/147/whm.html (accessed August 23, 2007).

[2] Nora Jaffary, "Gender and Race in Colonial Latin America," *Women in World History*, http://chnm.gmu.edu/wwh/d/124/wwh.html (accessed August 23, 2007).

Eric Allina-Pisano (EAP) is Associate Professor of International Development and Globalization and History at the University of Ottawa whose research interests include African history, colonial rule and globalization, slavery, and historical methods.

Joan Bristol (JB) is Associate Professor of History at George Mason University, specializing in colonial Latin America, comparative slavery, and historiography.

Benedict Carton (BC) is Associate Professor of History at George Mason University, specializing in Africa, health, environmental, global, imperial, and oral histories.

Michael Chang (MC) is Associate Professor of History at George Mason University, specializing in global, East Asian, and women's history.

Jack Cheng (JC) is an independent scholar based in Boston and a contributor to the *American Experience Online* and to the blog *The Public Humanist.*

Robert DeCaroli (RD) is Associate Professor of Art History at George Mason University, specializing in Buddhist art and early South Asian popular culture.

Robert Edgar (RE) is Professor of African Studies at Howard University with a focus on African history and culture, political history, and global world history.

Christopher K. Gardner (CG) teaches at Catholic University of America and Johns Hopkins University. His research interests include southern France, medieval urban culture, and the Crusades.

Anne Good (AG) is Assistant Professor of History at Reinhardt College in Georgia. Her research focuses on the intersections between early modern Germany and South Africa.

Mary Halavais (MH) is Associate Professor of History at Sonoma State University, specializing in early modern European history, Spain and Latin America as well as global history.

Sumaiya Hamdani (SAH) is Associate Professor at George Mason University. Her research interests include Islamic religion, law, and identity, women, and Islam in the modern Middle East.

Wayne Hanley (WH) is Associate Professor of History at West Chester University of Pennsylvania, specializing in modern European intellectual and cultural history with an emphasis on France, and methods of teaching secondary social studies.

Steven Harris (SH) is Assistant Professor of History at the University of Mary Washington, where he teaches courses on the history of modern Europe. His research focuses on Russia and the Soviet Union.

Mack Holt (MPH), Professor of History and Director of Graduate Studies, teaches at George Mason University. Holt's research interests encompass religious, political, social, and cultural history in early modern France.

Nora E. Jaffary (NJ) is Assistant Professor of History at Concordia University in Montreal, Canada whose current research focuses on the history of childbirth and contraception in colonial and nineteenth-century Mexico.

Matthew B. Karush (MK) is Associate Professor of History and Director of the Latin American Studies Program at George Mason University, and a specialist on modern Latin American labor and cultural history.

T. Mills Kelly (TMK) is Associate Director of the Center for History and New Media and Associate Professor of History at George Mason University, specializing in late-Habsburg history and Czech nationalism.

Christine Kray (CK) is Associate Professor of Anthropology at the Rochester Institute of Technology, specializing in Latin America, globalization, international migration, and social movements.

Kristin Day Lehner (KDL) is a graduate student in African history at Johns Hopkins University, where her research focuses on health and development in twentieth-century West Africa.

Patricia Lorcin (PL) is Associate Professor of History at the University of Minnesota, specializing in French imperialism and postcolonial studies.

John Bert Lott (JBL) is a professor in the Classics Department at Vassar College whose specialties include the Augustan Age of Rome, urbanism, and the interpretation of historical documents through new media.

Randolph H. Lytton (RL) is Associate Professor of History at George Mason University whose research interests in classical history include Alexander the Great, intellectual history, and historiography.

Kirsten McKenzie (KM) teaches at the University of Sydney in Australia. Her research interests include comparative British colonial identity focusing on the Cape Colony and New South Wales, gender issues, and the construction of celebrity.

Brian Platt (BP) is Associate Professor and Chair of the Department of History and Art History at George Mason University, focusing on the social and cultural history of Japan.

Jonathan Rotondo-McCord (JRM) is Associate Professor of History at Xavier University. His research interests are medieval Germany, social and church history, and comparative feudal structures in world history.

Kelly Schrum is Director of Educational Projects at the Center for History and New Media and an Associate Professor at George Mason University.

Nancy L. Stockdale (NS) is Assistant Professor at the University of North Texas. Her research interests include Middle Eastern history, with a special focus on women and gender, and world history.

We want to thank our funders, the National Endowment for the Humanities, The Gladys Krieble Delmas Foundation, George Mason University, and private donations, for generously supporting the development of the *World History Sources* and *Women in World History* websites. And a special thank you to Jenny Reeder, Ammon Shepherd, and Arminda Smith who helped in many ways with the research and creation of this book. Finally, we want to express our appreciation to Joan Feinberg, Mary Dougherty, Jane Knetzger, Kathryn Abbott, Louise Townsend, Katherine Flynn, and Lindsay DiGianvittorio at Bedford/St. Martin's who helped envision and shape this book.

Contents

World History Matters

A Student Guide to World History Online

1

An Introduction to World History Research Online

The sheer number and variety of historical resources available online today is truly remarkable. You can begin your study of ancient Egypt without leaving your computer by touring the Valley of the Kings, a burial ground for pharaohs of the New Kingdom in ancient Egypt, at the *Theban Mapping Project* [23]. You can then skip across the globe and forward in time several thousand years to watch Gandhi lead the "Salt March" in 1920 to protest the British tax on salt at the website *Harappa* [81]. Perhaps your research topic centers on Islamic ceramics, available through the *Topkapi Museum* website [65], or on cultural contact in the sixteenth century that you explore through European maps of the African continent, found on *Afriterra* [50] (Fig. 1). The Internet has become the most diverse, and the largest, repository of historical primary sources in the world. Millions of resources covering almost any subject of historical inquiry are readily available and can be used to examine the complexities of the past across time and space. These sources invite you to examine broad, cross-cultural interactions and

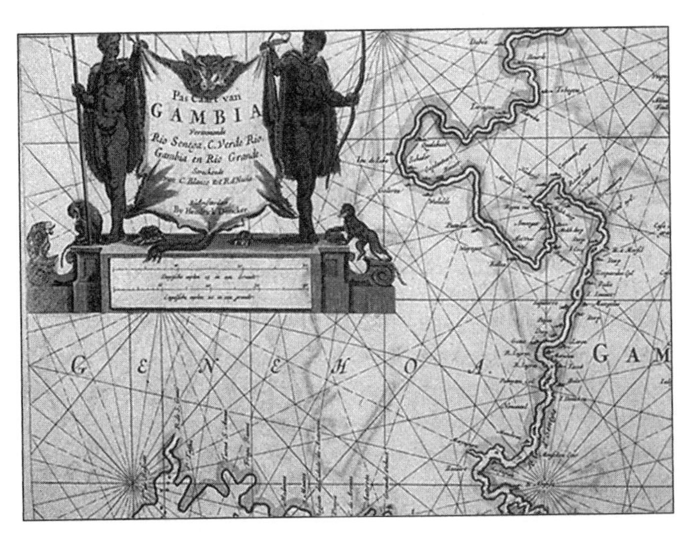

Fig. 1 Historical map from *Afriterra: The Cartographic Free Library* [50]. *(Historical Map, Hendrick Doncker, Amsterdam 1680. Courtesy of Afriterra Foundation, www.afriterra.org.)*

global trends, such as Irish migration (*Breaking the Silence* [132]) or trade along the Silk Road (*International Dunhuang Project* [32]), as well as specific people, times, or places, such as ancient Rome (*Virtual Catalog of Roman Coins* [30]) or Nelson Mandela (*ANC Historical Documents Archive* [129]). Or you can explore themes, such as travel narratives (*Women's Travel Writing, 1830–1930* [98] or *South Seas Voyaging and Cross-Cultural Encounters in the Pacific* [93]) and twentieth-century propaganda (*Chinese Propaganda Posters* [135] or *"A Summons To Comradeship": World War I and II Posters* [100]).

Not all websites are created equal, however, and the resources available online, especially in the field of world history, are uneven in quality. While they can offer valuable material previously inaccessible to many students, websites related to world history can also be the purveyors of misinformation, poorly translated texts, or biased narratives. World history online is also uneven in terms of regional and chronological coverage. For example, there are more websites devoted to European history than to African history or Latin American history. And while there are some excellent resources covering the period from the beginnings of human society through 1000 C.E. and even more from 1000 C.E. to the eighteenth century, the number of websites that focus on the past 300 years is significantly higher. It is relatively easy to find photographs, artifacts, and maps for studying world history; it is harder to find speeches, films, and oral histories. Many websites address art, popular culture, and religion, while fewer deal with health and disease or the environment.

Numbers alone, however, do not tell the whole story. The key is finding quality materials that relate to the specific theme or topic at hand. The *Thinker ImageBase* [15] presents more than 85,000 pieces of artwork from around the world, including paintings, photographs, furniture, pottery, and jewelry, dating from the sixth century B.C.E. to the twentieth century C.E. But if you are interested specifically in Buddhism, the *Huntington Archive of Buddhist and Related Art* [10] would be a better place to start, with thematically grouped images from Southeast and East Asia (Fig. 2). The *Index of Medieval Medical Images* [42] addresses a relatively narrow topic, but for a project on healing in the thirteenth and fourteenth centuries, it offers more than 500 high-quality images. *Vistas* [66] presents an even smaller number, roughly one hundred images. Each image, however, is accompanied by a discussion of its use, origin, and significance, along with thematic units that contextualize the images, provide background on "patterns of the every day," and discuss ways of making sense of pre-Columbian images. Depending on the course and the project, a smaller website like this one may prove most helpful.

Academics who study world history have been expanding their work from the study of societies in isolation to a focus on interactions and exchanges between cultures, a trend that has started to reshape the way world history is taught. Cross-cultural interactions are often at the heart of historical issues, and there are frequently multiple, conflicting accounts of any event or trend. Some of the websites listed in this book address cultural contact directly. Still others can be examined for evidence of cross-cultural contact even when it is not the

Fig. 2 Sculptural fragment of a Shiva figure from *Huntington Archive of Buddhist and Related Art* [10]. *(Head of Shiva, Cambodia, Style of Angkor Wat, 12th century. Tan sandstone, h. 42.0 cm. © The Cleveland Museum of Art, Purchase from the J.H. Wade Fund 1940.53.)*

website's explicit focus, allowing you to study the links between cultures, such as the dissemination of ideas from one society to another.

For example, *Atlantic Slave Trade and Slave Life in the Americas: A Visual Record* [52] intentionally presents cultures in contact, voluntarily and by force. This collection of 1,000 images of events, people, slave forts, and artifacts, such as ritual objects and punishment devices, encourages visitors to see slavery as an Atlantic system rather than a phenomenon limited to one region. In contrast, investigating cultural contact through *Japanese Old Photographs in Bakumatsu-Meiji Period* [84] requires a more conscious effort. The website displays 5,000 hand-tinted photographs dating from the second half of the nineteenth century. Taken primarily by Western diplomats, missionaries, and merchants, these images portray Japanese people and society during a period of rapid transformation, modernization, and confrontation with Western imperialism. The photographs also reveal Western perspectives, focusing on an exotic Japan, full of shrines, pagodas, and geisha. To explore clothing, architecture, or the emerging technology of photography, these images could be examined alongside other photographs from the late nineteenth century, such as those taken by American photographer William Henry Jackson during his tour of North Africa, Asia, Australia, and Oceania in the 1890s [71], or those found in the *Abdul-Hamid II Collection Photography Archive* [67] of late-nineteenth-century photographs from the Ottoman Empire.

To help you find the best websites for your project, *World History Matters* provides a roadmap for locating reliable sources quickly as well as a series of important questions to ask when you find them. Whatever your assignment or interests, you are sure to find valuable resources awaiting further exploration. The Internet can help you track down answers to historical questions or explore fascinating primary sources to challenge traditional explanations in world history. Use it wisely and it can be a valuable tool for learning about the past.

Evaluating Websites

One of the greatest strengths of the Internet is its egalitarianism — anyone can post anything online. When it comes to historical research, this egalitarianism is both a strength and a weakness. On the positive side, it means that a rich, diverse pool of historical primary sources is available to anyone who is interested in them. On the negative side, far too many websites containing primary sources are of questionable quality. There are several essential questions to ask when assessing a website's reliability — questions you need to answer before you start to use the primary sources found within.

Who Created the Website?

The first thing you need to know about any website you plan to use is who is responsible for its content. Who selected the sources presented there? How are they presented? Who is providing the financial support for the project? Sometimes the authorship of a website is easily determined. As you can see in this screenshot, *The Word on the Street* [99], a collection of broadsides from Scotland, was created by the National Library of Scotland (Fig. 3). At the bottom of the page are links to the National Library of Scotland, National Library of Scotland Digital Library, and credits. Similarly, *Famous Trials* [8] clearly states at the top of the home page that the site was created "by Douglas O. Linder (2007) University of Missouri–Kansas City (UMKC) School of Law" (Fig. 4). It also provides a link to Linder's other web creations and biographical information. Knowing that the website is the work of a professor whose professional work is directly related to the content of the website will help you to judge both the quality of the sources *and* the quality of any interpretations presented.

In contrast, incomplete or non-existent credit information is a clue that a website may not be reliable. For instance, if you type "Adolf Hitler" into a popular

Fig. 3 Screenshot from *The Word on the Street* [99]. *(The Word on the Street. Used with permission by The Trustees of the National Library of Scotland.)*

Fig. 4 Screenshot from *Famous Trials* [8]. *(Famous Trials. Image provided and permission granted by Doug Linder, UMKC School of Law.)*

search engine, one of the top results is the *Hitler Historical Museum*, **http://www.hitler.org**. This website contains a number of interesting primary sources from Adolf Hitler's life and career, but it is impossible to determine who put them there. A careful reading of the contents reveals that the author(s) believe that Hitler has been unfairly criticized by historians. For example, a link to "Adolf Hitler Books" is accompanied by the comment: "Translation of Third Reich Originals without snide commentary." As a general rule, controversial topics require extra investigation and a very careful reading of the contextual material on the website. Be especially skeptical if (a) a topic is very controversial; (b) you cannot determine who the author is; and (c) you find obvious biases.

Most websites offer an "About" page with information describing the website and its creator(s) or, at a minimum, a contact email address. Even a lone email address may provide a clue to the authorship of the website. Is it based at a university (*e.g.*, someone@gmu.edu) or a government agency (*e.g.*, someone@loc.gov)? Or does it come from a commercial email provider such as *Hotmail*?

Another way to puzzle out who is responsible for a website is to shorten the URL. Try deleting the text after the last forward slash (/) and pressing *Enter* on your keyboard. For example, if you were looking at *The Avalon Project: Documents in Law, History, and Diplomacy* [4], **http://www.yale.edu/lawweb/avalon/avalon.htm**, you would delete *avalon.htm* which takes you back to the *Avalon* home page. When you delete the last two sections of the URL, *avalon/avalon.htm*, you are directed to the Yale University Law School. Deleting further takes you to Yale University's home page, **www.yale.edu**. Yale University and its School of Law are well-respected institutions that lend credibility to *The Avalon Project* and the material it provides.

In other cases, shortening the URL may not help. Not every URL that ends in *.edu* is officially sanctioned by an educational institution. Students and faculty often have access to URLs that are on their institution's server. So **http://www.ucla.edu/~jones** might be the URL for someone named Jones who is affiliated with the University of California at Los Angeles, but it is not necessarily run as an official university website. In addition, many websites are now built on databases with long and complex URLs that may lead to a central webserver at a large organization, such as a government agency. Or they may only lead to hosting services that offer no hints to the background of the website creator.

Once upon a time in the history of the Internet it was possible to make some judgments about a website based upon its domain name. URLs issued in the United States that ended in *.com* signified commercial purposes, those ending in *.org* were intended for non-commercial purposes, and those ending in *.net* were intended for network providers. Today, however, any organization or individual can purchase a *.com, .net, .org, .biz, .tv*, or *.us* domain name, so these suffixes do not necessarily indicate who is responsible for a website. And outside the United States, domain names end with a two letter code signifying the country where the website is based — or at least where the domain name was sold. Thus, an address ending in *.uk* is based in the United Kingdom and one ending in *.ch* is based in Switzerland. The exceptions to this free market in domain names are those based in the United States that are reserved for specific uses: *.edu* for educational institutions in the U.S., *.mil* for the U.S. military, and *.gov* for the U.S. government. So, for instance, websites based at American colleges, universities, and schools all end in *.edu* and those at government institutions, such as the Department of State or National Archives, end in *.gov*.

Where Did the Sources on the Website Come From?

The next important question to ask when you want to use web-based sources responsibly is about the origin of the materials provided. The website *Excerpts from Slave Narratives* [77], created by Steven Mintz at the University of Houston, offers 46 first-person accounts of slavery and African life dating from 1682 to 1937. A source citation for each account is listed at the end of the text. For example, the narrative of Venture Smith includes the following note: "A Narrative of the Life and Adventures of Venture, A Native of Africa (New London, Conn., 1798; expanded ed., Hamden, Conn., 1896)." The original source citations are particularly important in this case because the website offers *excerpts*. The citation allows you to track down the full source and read the entire narrative. By contrast, the *Hitler Historical Museum* mentioned earlier offers no source information for the speeches and photographs provided, making verification impossible.

Have the Sources Been Altered in Any Way?

The slave narrative example leads to a follow-up question: Is the website presenting the source in its entirety or just a portion of the source? Has the source been edited or otherwise changed? That question is relevant whether the source is a text, object, image, or video clip. In the case of text, website creators such as Mintz often, but not always, inform you that the text you are reading is an excerpt. In other cases, the text will contain ellipses (. . .) to indicate that portions of the complete text have been cut.

When looking at an image, though, it is harder to determine if something is an original or has been cropped or changed. Image editing tools make alterations simple and edited photographs can look authentic. First, check to see if the creators discuss this issue anywhere on the website. Second, ask yourself if anything about the image might suggest that it has been altered. Do the colors seem unnatural? Have you seen other versions of this image that included features or people not in the current one? Similar questions hold true for video and audio sources, especially with the increasing popularity of online media. Does an audio or video clip seem edited or complete? Are there unnatural moments or cuts that might indicate editing or deletions? If anything in the source gives you pause, look for a more complete version.

Fig. 5a

Fig. 5b

Compare these two photographs carefully. Do you notice any differences? The man with the glasses who is touching his hat is missing from the second image (Fig. 5b). The first image (Fig. 5a) was taken shortly after the Russian Revolution. In the center of the photograph, it shows two of the key leaders: V. I. Lenin (left) and Leon Trotsky (right). After Lenin's death on January 21, 1924, a power struggle ensued to determine who would assume leadership of the Soviet Union (U.S.S.R.). Joseph Stalin emerged as the winner of this struggle and by 1929 had solidified his place as Lenin's successor. He then had Trotsky expelled from the

U.S.S.R. and later assassinated, and erased his name and image from the written and visual records of the revolution. To achieve this, the photograph's negative was retouched to remove Trotsky. Finding an alternate version allows you to compare and to see how the original was altered.[1]

How Current is the Website?

Another important question is currency — currency of the website and currency of the materials presented on the website. Was the website created in 1999, but recently updated? Or was it created in 2004 with no revisions? Older websites that are not maintained generally have problems such as broken links. Currency may also matter because recent research can shed new light on historical questions or translations. Copyright permission to use recent English translations can be very expensive, so in the interest of presenting a wide body of materials, some websites, such as *Perseus Digital Library* [27] and the *Internet History Sourcebooks Project* [11] generally present translations created before 1923. These are valuable materials, but new research and more recent translations are often available in books and should be consulted for in-depth projects. On the other hand, an unchanging website might present the most recent sources available on your topic.

Assessing the significance of this issue requires knowledge about the state of research on your topic — information that can be found in secondary sources, especially in books in your library. Take, for example, a website devoted to the history of China. If the website was created in 1998 and has not been updated since, it would not reflect China's rapid economic growth in the past decade. If your topic is ancient China, the lack of updates might not affect your research. If you are interested in manufacturing trends over the past hundred years, however, recent updates would be very important. Information about the date of creation and date of revision for a website is often provided at the bottom of the homepage or on the "About" page.

Does the Website Present a Particular Perspective, Bias, or Agenda?

A common way to locate online resources is via search engines that lead you to a specific page within a website, bypassing the homepage. Before using a resource from an internal page, though, visit the homepage. It will help you answer the final questions you need to ask before using a website for research. The first is whether the resources available on the website are appropriate to the subject of the website. If the website is devoted to the history of European imperialism in sub-Saharan Africa, then one would expect to find sources from *both* the European and African sides of the story. It is rarely the case that websites are this comprehensive, though. More commonly, they tell one side of the story or

[1]See *Material Culture: Images, "How was the image made?"* on *World History Sources*, **http://chnm.gmu.edu/worldhistorysources/unpacking/imageexq3.php** (accessed July 17, 2007).

the other, as in *Formosa: Nineteenth Century Images* [78]. This website provides excellent resources from the perspective of European and American travelers to Taiwan, but you need to look elsewhere to find Taiwanese or Chinese views. A homepage should provide a clear sense of the scope of materials available on that particular website and the goals of the creator(s).

One last question is whether the creators of the website have a particular ideological, religious, or analytical agenda and how that agenda might shape the selection of resources. The *Noble Qur'an* [34], for example, is sponsored by the Muslim Student Association, a national organization founded by the Wahhabi Sunni sect (the official sect of Saudi Arabia). The organization has a specific goal: to provide religious guidance to Muslim students on U.S. university campuses. Yet it also provides excellent primary sources for those studying Islam — three full, scholarly translations of the Qur'an (or Koran) along with transliterations, introductions to each chapter, and background essays. Understanding a website's agenda helps you assess the resources and use them in an informed way.

Web 2.0

Now that we have covered the main questions to ask as you locate historical resources online, we want to discuss two recent developments in digital history related to Web 2.0. Web 2.0 refers to a new generation of web applications, such as wikis and social networking websites, that allow for and encourage collaboration and active participation among users. Web 2.0 developments impact history classrooms and historical research in many ways, and as with the Internet in general, are most valuable when we understand and assess their strengths and weaknesses.

The first development is the advent of websites based on *wiki* technologies. Wikis (the word comes from the Polynesian phrase *wiki-wiki* or *quick-quick*) are software platforms that allow anyone to add or edit content on the website at any time. The most heavily trafficked website with historical information is *Wikipedia*, **http://en.wikipedia.org**, providing background information on close to two million English-language topics (Fig. 6). It is commonly used for research on historical background by students, either with or without approval from their teachers. But it is important to remember that each entry in *Wikipedia* is the collective work of multiple authors. You can see the screen name or IP address of the various authors and editors for a given entry by looking at the history tab, a list of all versions of the entry and the changes made (Fig. 7). You may or may not be able to verify the identity or credentials of a given author with this information, however, often making it difficult to validate the authority of the entry.

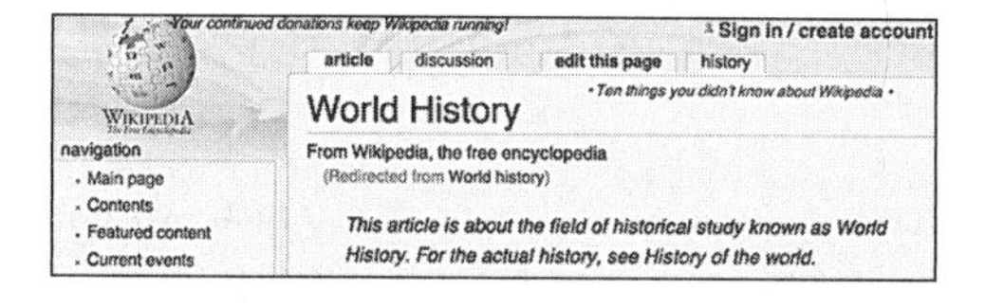

Fig. 6 Screenshot from *Wikipedia*, "World History" entry. *(World History screenshot, Wikipedia, August 28, 2007. www.wikipedia.org.)*

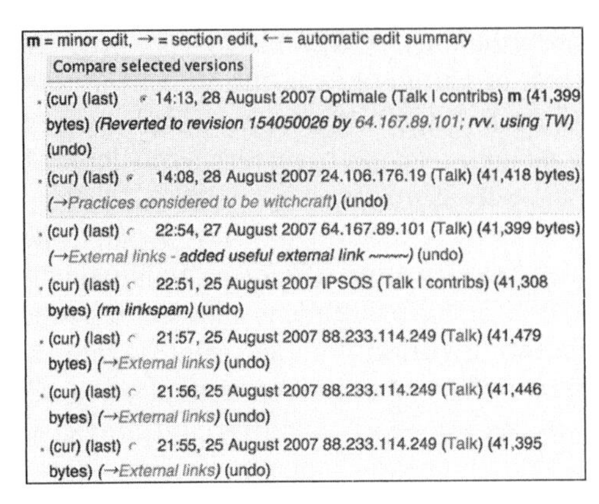

Fig. 7 Screenshot from *Wikipedia*, "Witchcraft" history tab. *(Witchcraft screenshot, Wikipedia, August 28, 2007. www.wikipedia.org.)*

So how do you know if an author is sharing knowledge, repeating rumors, or posting incorrect information?

Critics reject *Wikipedia* outright as inaccurate because its entries, unlike those in traditional encyclopedias, are the work of both non-experts and experts on a given subject. Supporters argue that *Wikipedia* produces a collective wisdom that is, for the most part, accurate, and that having multiple authors increases the likelihood that someone will catch errors. Both sides raise valid points. Comparisons of entries in *Wikipedia* to those in more traditional encyclopedias like the *Encyclopedia Brittanica* do turn up errors, but the errors appear in both the traditional print encyclopedias and *Wikipedia*. *Wikipedia* entries on popular topics — such as Charles Darwin or the Taj Mahal, for instance — are often just as accurate as those in conventional encyclopedias.[2]

To use *Wikipedia* wisely, there are two things to keep in mind. The first is that *Wikipedia* is a collectively authored *encyclopedia*. *Wikipedia* does not value original research; indeed, it prohibits it. Encyclopedias are useful for looking up facts, but they contain little or no interpretation of those facts. The second, given the ever-changing nature of *Wikipedia*, is that *when* you visit an entry matters. Five minutes after your visit, the information may be substantially altered and may even earn the *Wikipedia* warning, "The neutrality and factual accuracy of this article are disputed" as posted on the entry for the Indian Independence Movement on August 28, 2007 (Fig. 8). To cite a *Wikipedia* entry, include the date and time, available on the "History" tab, to identify which version you used.

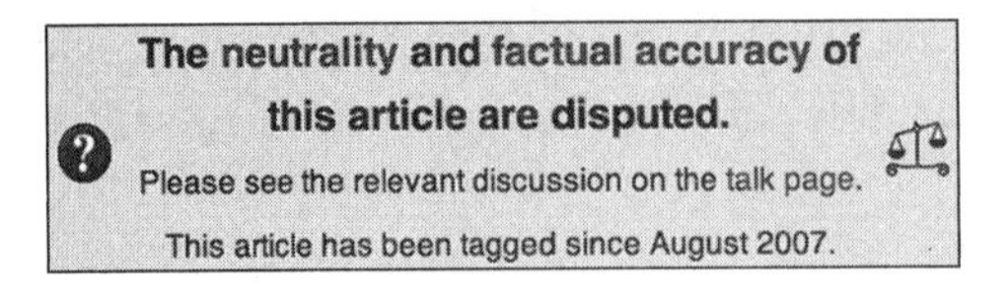

Fig. 8 Screenshot from *Wikipedia*, "Indian Independence Movement" entry. *(Indian Independence Movement screenshot, Wikipedia, August 28, 2007. www.wikipedia.org.)*

[2]Roy Rosenzweig, "Can History be Open Source? Wikipedia and the Future of the Past," reprinted from *The Journal of American History* 93, no.1 (June 2006), **http://chnm.gmu.edu/resources/essays/d/42** (accessed July 13, 2007).

A second Web 2.0 development is changing the way we do historical research online. Social networking databases such as the photo-sharing website *Flickr.com* or the video-sharing website *YouTube.com* include new historical content every day. Users of these websites with an interest in the past post historical images and films, such as World War II newsreels, from multiple countries. One significant downside to using this kind of historical material is that it rarely includes any source information, making it difficult or impossible to locate originals or verify origin. On the other hand, these websites often contain material not commonly available. For instance, if you wanted to compare political graffiti across societies or over time, *Flickr.com* might be an excellent resource. Users around the world have made available tens of thousands of photographs of graffiti that otherwise would be inaccessible without extensive travel, and are unlikely to be included in a traditional online archive (Fig. 9).

Most Web 2.0 sites allow users to interact with content and with each other by editing material directly (as in the case of *Wikipedia*) or by commenting on what they see, read, or watch. The commentary is unlikely to relate to your research, but on occasion, comments can help you make sense of an image or film clip or provide a personal experience connected with it. You may also find visitors to the website who share your interest or who might have expertise that would help you answer a question. As with the sources themselves, though, proceed with caution and verify authenticity.

History students are taking part in these Web 2.0 developments every day and in the process are participating in the creation of historical content in new ways. Some instructors, for example, require their students to create and edit entries in *Wikipedia*, both because it teaches students about the pros and cons of this online encyclopedia and because it teaches them about the creation of historical information in a public forum. Other students create and edit *Wikipedia* entries on their own because they have an interest in the subject matter. In this way they are taking part in the creation of our common fund of historical knowledge.

Fig. 9 Vivitar graffiti from *Flickr.com*. *(Vivitar Graffiti, Permission granted by photographer, David Ross.)*

Even more common is the posting of photographs and video files on *Flickr.com* or *YouTube.com*. Although the vast majority of the material posted to these websites by history students has nothing to do with history, a growing fraction is historical in nature — photographs of memorial sites such as monuments or battlegrounds, or video files that include material from earlier decades, such as clips from news broadcasts of significant events such as the Tiananmen Square protest and massacre in 1989.

Working with Online Primary and Secondary Sources

What is a primary source? What is a secondary source? Knowing the difference between the two categories of materials about the past is important. While both are valuable and useful, they provide different kinds of information and therefore are used in different ways.

Primary sources are materials directly related to the past by time or participation — things created in the past by people living at the time. Historians build their analyses of people, places, and events from these pieces of the past. The category "primary source" includes photographs, prints, paintings, government documents, advertisements, religious emblems, musical recordings, speeches by politicians, films, letters (by ordinary as well as by famous people), newspaper articles, sermons, and material culture such as pottery, furniture, or tools. Primary sources provide the opportunity to engage directly with the past, to try to sort out what happened and why. Working with historical primary sources, however, is not easy. Evidence from the past represents individual experiences as well as social exchanges, and its meaning is rarely obvious at first glance.

Secondary sources are interpretations, syntheses, or descriptions of the past created by a historian or writer who has studied a range of primary sources and read other secondary sources. For example, a page from the manuscript *Nueva corónica y buen gobierno* or *New Chronicle and Good Government* written by native Andean Felipe Guamán Poma de Ayala in 1615 [58] is a primary source. An article by a historian analyzing the manuscript to discuss Andean history or the effects of Spanish colonization on indigenous people is a secondary source. As with websites, secondary sources reflect the author's point of view, shaping what primary sources will be included and how they will be interpreted.

In most cases, the distinction between primary and secondary sources is clear. In some situations, though, the lines are blurred. A textbook is generally considered a secondary source. In the twenty-first century, however, we might use a textbook from 1960 as a primary source to research what students learned about the Cold War or to what degree history textbooks discussed women's roles in historic events a half century ago.

Oral history presents another complicated case. Oral histories are usually collected years and even decades after the events being discussed, so they are both a history of the past and a record of how that past has been remembered. The *Uysal-Walker Archive of Turkish Oral Narrative* [149], for example, presents Turkish folktales that reflect oral traditions created during and after the Otto-

Primary Sources and Secondary Sources

Primary Sources	Secondary Sources
A photograph of armed men and women during the Mexican Revolution	Analysis of the photograph or the photographer in a history journal
A travel journal	A book written by a leading historian in the twenty-first century about nineteenth-century travel writing
An official document such as the Peace Treaty of Versailles	A recording of a college lecture about the end of World War I
A 1931 advertisement for Electrolux vacuum cleaners from *New Zealand Free Lance* magazine	A website on the rise of advertising in the twentieth century or on the changing roles of women and nature of work in the home
A 1970 poster reading "Stop Collaboration: Support Resistance in Southern South Africa"	A scholarly essay about the anti-apartheid movement
A musical recording of a New Mexican wedding song	A Library of Congress website about music sung by Spanish-speaking residents in northern New Mexico and southern Colorado
A Portuguese map of America drawn in 1580	A modern map showing sixteenth-century Portuguese colonies
The fifteenth-century tax survey record for a 56-year-old woman named Alessandra Buondelmon	A study of the 10,000 tax records collected in 1427 that analyzes individual, family, and economic trends in Florence, Italy.
A children's toy from Ancient Mesopotamia	A textbook discussion of daily life in the Middle East in the Ancient World.

man Empire. These were collected over a period of forty years in the late twentieth century. They are primary sources, but must be analyzed while keeping the process of collection, elapsed time, and role of memory in mind.

When working with primary and secondary sources, it is important to understand that history is not a simple, fixed narrative. Historians debate, discuss, and even disagree about the meaning of various sources and interpretations of the past. Many factors shape historical events and historians also look at how things might have happened given different circumstances or when seen through another pair of eyes. For example, our understanding of history changes when we look at the experiences of political leaders versus the daily lives of those who were not known nationally or internationally. Looking at multiple perspectives can provide a more complex understanding of the past. In addition, learning to understand the past, to connect it to a larger story, is key. Equally important is the skill of investigating the past carefully and with an open mind, allowing yourself to see things that may not fit with the larger narrative you have learned.

There are dozens, hundreds, or even millions of primary sources available on almost any subject in world history. Think about what kinds of sources are most relevant to your project and then start with background research. Are there just a few resources available? Can you review them all? What if there are hundreds or thousands of sources on your topic, such as the more than 2,000 documents in the *Marxists Internet Archive* [115]. To begin, you could select a sample of the total or focus on one time period or a single author. The website *PictureAustralia* [119] presents a vast collection of 600,000 images documenting Australia's cultural history — far too many to use in a single research project. However, a search on "child" returns forty-one images — a much more manageable number that would allow you to begin to explore childhood, indigenous people, and colonization.

Here are several important steps historians take when analyzing a primary source.

Sourcing: Who created the source and what do we know about that person or group of people? When and where did it appear? What happened to it after its first appearance? What can we learn about an author's motives, intentions, or point of view? Is the creator in a position to be a good reporter? Why or why not? How did the source survive? Why is it available in the twenty-first century?

Close Reading: Start by carefully reading or analyzing the source. For a written document, consider the kind of source, tone, and word choice. Pay attention to parts of speech — what kinds of nouns or adjectives are used? Does this remain consistent throughout the document or does it change? How formal or informal is the language? Is the account believable? Is it internally consistent or are there contradictions? For an image, look carefully at each section separately and then look at the whole. Listen to a song or watch a video multiple times. What does the source say or look like or sound like? What might it mean? What does each section mean? How do the sections work together? What questions come up as you carefully analyze the source itself?

Contextualization: Consider the larger historical picture and situate the source within a framework of events and perspectives, paying close attention to *when* they happened and *where* they took place. When was the source created? What else was happening at this time that may have influenced the creator? Where was this source created? How might location have influenced its creation? How might an intended or unintended audience have shaped the source?

Corroboration: Whenever possible, check important details against each other. Evaluate multiple sources in relationship to one another, and look for similarities as well as contradictions. Look at key content and stylistic differences. Where do the sources agree with one another? Where do they disagree? What viewpoint does each source reflect? Which sources seem more reliable or trustworthy? Why?

The *World History Matters* website, **http://worldhistorymatters.org**, offers some additional resources for learning to analyze different kinds of primary sources. Eight guides offer strategies for analyzing particular types of primary sources (music, images, objects, maps, newspapers, travel narratives, official documents, and personal accounts) as part of world history. Historian Jerry Bentley, for example, discusses a set of questions to ask when working with travel narratives, such as: "Who is the author of the travel account?" "What kinds of interests motivated the traveler and the author of the travel account?" and "What influence has the travel account had during its own and later times?" In addition, in sixteen multimedia case studies, scholars model strategies for interpreting primary sources and placing them in historical context. Historian Joan Bristol analyzes a record from the Mexican Inquisition and unravels the story of Gertrudis de Escobar, a 14-year-old *mulata* servant who was accused of renouncing God. Bristol discusses the use of Inquisition records in investigating youth, race, and religion in seventeenth-century New Spain.[3]

Many websites also contain secondary source content. This may include explanatory or contextualizing text that introduces the topic, explains a particular source, or leads to a bibliography of related scholarly articles and books. These secondary source materials provide both a context for understanding the sources and an entry point into the conversation that historians are having about a particular topic. *Vindolanda Tablets Online* [29] for example, presents close to 1,000 wooden writing tablets found at the Roman auxiliary fortress at Vindolanda behind Hadrian's Wall in Britain. These tablets from the late first and early second centuries C.E., discarded by departing troops, record official and personal accounts of life in one community of the Roman world. The "exhibition," a valuable secondary source, introduces this rather unique find, discussing Vindolanda and its setting, the history of Roman forts, the lives of soldiers, the community at large, background on the documents and process of translation, and strategies for reading the texts. This information provides a framework and strategies for beginning to understand a source that was created a long time ago, in a language no longer spoken. When you begin to analyze the primary sources yourself, you can take part in that conversation.

Search Tips and Further Resources

Using Search Engines Effectively

Browsing is very helpful when you are starting a project and do not have a specific resource or topic in mind. A well-designed website allows you to wander around large thematic or chronological sections, to see connections and groupings. When you do know what you want, however, a keyword search is

[3]Jerry Bentley, "Travel Narratives," *World History Sources*, **http://chnm.gmu.edu/worldhistorysources/unpacking/travelmain.html** (accessed August 23, 2007); Joan Bristol, "Inquisition Documents," *Women in World History*, **http://chnm.gmu.edu/wwh/analyzing/documents/docs.intro.php** (accessed August 22, 2007).

sometimes the best path. *Google*, the most commonly used search engine, can be a powerful tool, especially once you understand how it works and how to use it wisely.

The first wave of search engines, such as *AltaVista*, *HotBot*, and *Excite*, were not very successful at discriminating between high-quality and low-quality websites. A poorly written website that mentioned the Holocaust fifty times might be mechanically ranked more "relevant" than an authoritative website from the *United States Holocaust Memorial Museum* [124] that mentioned the word only a dozen times on its home page. In the late 1990s, *Google* revolutionized the way search engines work, presenting a smarter search engine.

Google, for example, looks at the presence of keywords in the title and URL rather than searching meta tags, the hidden tags written by a website author to describe the contents of a webpage. The more significant development, however, built upon a unique element of the web itself — the ability to link to other websites. *Google* founders Larry Page and Sergey Brin found a way to use the popularity of certain websites to promote their rankings. A website on the Holocaust with twenty links to it from other websites was probably better than a site with one or two links to it. If in turn some of those other websites were "authoritative" (*i.e.*, they also had lots of links to them), so much the better for the first website's ranking. In short, *Google* found a way to measure reputation on the web through a recursive analysis of the interconnectedness of the medium itself.[4]

Here are some additional tips for finding what you are looking for.

Use Quotation Marks Using quotation marks makes your search more specific by identifying multiple search terms as a specific phrase. If you enter the words *world history* without quotes, *Google* returns more than 800 million results. If you put the search term in quotes ("world history") you have just narrowed it down to two and a half million. Entering the specific topic, time period, or region you are interested in exploring, such as "world history" "Latin America," will narrow it still further.

Use Advanced Search The easiest way to expedite your search and quickly move from millions of returns to hundreds or even dozens, is to use the Advanced Search feature. You can click on "Advanced Search" from the main search page or go directly to **http://www.google.com/advanced_search**. This allows you to narrow your search to specific languages, include or exclude words or phrases, restrict domain names, or define the location of occurrences (*e.g.*, the phrase occurs anywhere on the page, only in the title, or only in the text of a webpage).

Enter Multiple Terms If you are interested in the role played by American troops in the Boxer Rebellion, you'll want to enter "boxer rebellion American troops," since anything else might take you to a website on Mohammed Ali. The

[4]Daniel J. Cohen and Roy Rosenzweig, "Building an Audience: Mass Marketing, Online and Off," *Digital History: A Guide to Gathering, Preserving, and Presenting the Past on the Web*, University of Pennsylvania Press, **http://chnm.gmu.edu/digitalhistory/audience/2.php** (accessed July 16, 2007).

first website returned by the *Google* search engine in this search is the *Wikipedia* page on the Boxer Rebellion. The second website is from the National Archives and offers an article (secondary source) on the involvement of American troops in the Rebellion. The third choice is from the Public Broadcasting Service (PBS), and includes the transcript of an interview with noted American diplomatic historian Walter LaFeber. The fourth is from *About.com* which simply republishes the content from *Wikipedia*. It is not until you get to the ninth choice in the *Google* search that you finally have access to primary sources, in this case drawn from the collections of the U.S. Navy.

Tell Google *Where to Find It* If you know that you saw a sixteenth-century map of Casablanca on the website *Historic Cities: Maps and Documents* [60] but you do not remember how you found it, you can type your keyword and the URL "casablanca site:historic-cities.huji.ac.il" into a *Google* search and the map will be your first hit. If you remember that the title of a website you visited included the words "digital," "Islamic," and "project" you can type "intitle:digital islamic project" to quickly find the *Ahlul-Bayt Digital Islamic Library Project* [31].

Other such operators include *intext:*, *allintext:*, *allintitle:*, *inurl:*, *author:*, and *location:*.

Use the +, –, |, and ~ Signs It is also possible to limit the results of a *Google* search by using special characters. If you are interested in listening directly to the words of Agatha Christie or Salmon Rushdie, you might search for "Agatha Christie" + "audio" or "Salmon Rushdie" + "audio" to quickly find their interviews on *BBC Audio Interviews* [131]. The minus sign (–) means *not* and the solid vertical line (|) substitutes for *or*. So if you are searching for information on the John Scopes trial, you might try "John Scopes | monkey + trial" because the trial was also called the "Monkey" trial. Or, if you wanted search results that *excluded Wikipedia*, you would use "John Scopes | monkey – wikipedia" to access more carefully selected search results. If you are not sure about different names for the same thing, try using the synonym search. Using the (~) symbol in your search returns the term you are looking for *and* any synonyms of that term.

Translate a Text Although a rough translator at best, *Google* can give you the "gist" of an article or website in a number of languages, including Arabic, Chinese, French, German, Italian, Japanese, Korean, Russian, Portuguese, or Spanish. See **http://www.google.com/language_tools** for this feature. Beware, however, that free, online translations are often imperfect.

Link Check An additional tool for assessing the reliability of a website is investigating which other websites and organizations find it valuable. Run a "link check" on *Google* by typing "link" and the complete URL into the *Google* search field as follows:

link:http://www.giftsofspeech.org

The link check on *Gifts of Speech: Women's Speeches from Around the World* [140], created by Sweet Briar College, yields 165 items. This means that more than

150 websites link directly to this archive. Even more promising, many of these links come from library, teaching, and university websites, indicating that an academic audience has favorably reviewed this website.

Other Searches Did you know that you can find a current map by typing an address into *Google* or using *Google Maps*, **http://maps.google.com**? You can also find out what a word means by asking *Google*. For example, you can find out the two possible meanings of *portmanteau* by entering "define:portmanteau." You can convert measurements or make a calculation with *Google*. Type "9000/4" and *Google* will return the answer "2250." Type "35 degrees Celsius in Fahrenheit" and you will receive "95 degrees Fahrenheit."

Other Search Engines When searching for information on current events, you may want to search directly on media websites such as the *New York Times*, **http://www.nytimes.com**, or the *British Broadcasting System*, **http://www.bbc.co.uk**. Both offer broad coverage of current events, although access to archived articles is not free. You can also try other search engines such as *Metacrawler*, **http://www.metacrawler.com**, and *Vivísimo*, **http://www.vivisimo.com**. Keep a library of "favorites" or "bookmarks" with search engines or websites that you use frequently for research.

A Word About Plagiarism

Printed materials have long provided ready content for plagiarism, but the Internet, and the mixture of skill and naiveté with which many approach it, creates new opportunities and new dangers. Online texts, images, sounds, and videos are easy to copy, paste, and manipulate. While this may make note taking easier, it also makes plagiarism — intentional or unintentional — as easy as clicking on "copy" and "paste." Many students are not aware of the full meaning of plagiarism and its repercussions. School and college policies vary, but students who are caught plagiarizing can encounter a range of consequences, from failing a course to expulsion. Plagiarism does not have to be deliberate to be wrong — unintentional plagiarism is generally subject to the same penalties.[5]

Plagiarism is presenting the words, work, or opinions of someone else as one's own without proper acknowledgment. This includes borrowing the sequence of ideas, the arrangement of material, or the pattern of thought from someone else without proper acknowledgment. If a history paper gives the impression that the writer of the paper is the author of the words, ideas, or conclusions when they are the product of another person's work, the writer of that paper is guilty of plagiarism. This is equally true for published and unpublished materials (such as a paper written by another student) as well as for any material found on the Internet.

[5]Johns Hopkins University History Department guidelines; Diana Hacker, *The Bedford Handbook for Writers*, 4th ed. (New York: St. Martin's, 1994), 477–479; *Bedford/St. Martin's Workshop on Plagiarism*, **bedfordstmartins.com/plagiarism/flyer**.

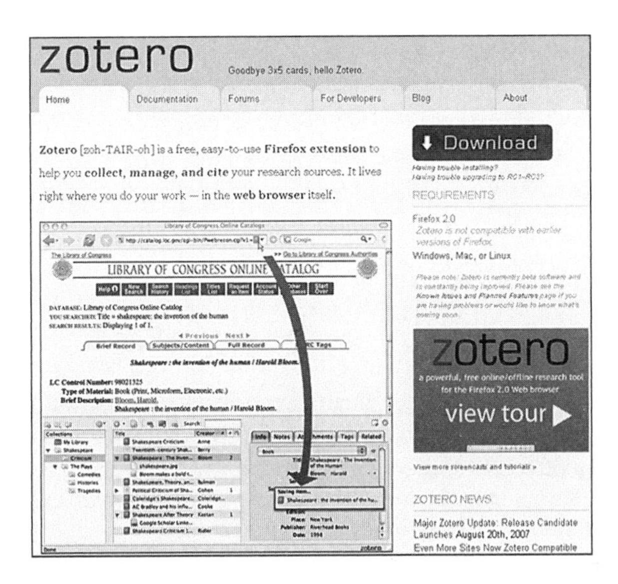

Fig. 10 Screenshot from *Zotero*. *(Permission granted by Center for History and New Media, George Mason University.)*

Studying other people's ideas through primary and secondary sources is central to conducting historical research. Historians use quotations from primary sources to illustrate their arguments and include quotations from other scholars to place their discussion in a larger context. Both of these uses are acceptable, and indeed desirable, aspects of writing a history paper. The key is to always credit the source of direct quotations, paraphrased information, or ideas and to use your skills to create your own original ideas and historical analysis.

There are new tools to help you in this process. *Zotero*, **http://www.zotero.org**, a free extension for the popular open-source web browser *Firefox*, allows you to build, organize, and annotate your own collections while conducting research online (Fig. 10). With the click of a mouse, it collects and saves all available reference information about a website, book, article, or other primary source from major research websites and databases, such as *JSTOR*, *ProQuest*, and *Google Books*, as well as most library catalogs. Once saved into *Zotero*, you can add notes, drag and drop texts and images into multiple collections (folders), search your collections, export citations, and create "reports" or documents summarizing your research. You can also highlight and add notes to stored documents from the Web. Tools such as *Zotero* help you organize your research and reduce the risk of ending up with unidentified sources or notes, a key factor in avoiding plagiarism.[6]

[6]For more information, see Daniel J. Cohen, "Zotero: Social and Semantic Computing for Historical Scholarship," *Perspectives* (May 2007), **http://www.historians.org/Perspectives/issues/2007/0705/0705tec2.cfm** (accessed June 29, 2007).

Here are some steps that you can take to avoid plagiarism.

1) Start by taking notes carefully, especially when moving from a website to a word processing document or when typing notes from a book. If you copy and paste, always put the entire text in quotes and include the full citation. If you paraphrase, make sure that you understand the original text and then put it aside. Write the idea in your own words and be sure to cite the author as the source of the idea, even when it is not a direct quote.
2) When you quote directly from a source to a computer document (including all citation information), change the color of the quote with your word processor to make it stand out from the rest of the text. This will serve as a visual reminder that something is a quote and requires proper citation.
3) Update your list of sources, primary and secondary, as you take notes. Use the guidelines for citing electronic resources listed below.
4) Keep a copy of each source you use, including photocopies of print articles and key passages from books. Print copies of online sources or email them to yourself and store them together in one folder.
5) Save drafts of your work as you research and write papers. When you begin to make revisions, create a new copy and save the original. This creates a record of your work and the development of your thoughts.
6) Finally, learn more about plagiarism, paraphrasing, and college regulations by visiting a writing center or library. Visit the websites listed below for additional definitions, suggestions, and resources.

Additional Online Resources on Research, Plagiarism, and Documenting Sources:

Research and Documentation Online, Diana Hacker
http://dianahacker.com/resdoc

Writer's Handbook, University of Wisconsin-Madison, Writing Center
http://www.wisc.edu/writing/Handbook

Documenting Sources, George Mason University Writing Center
http://writingcenter.gmu.edu/resources/plagiarism.html

Citing Online Sources

Citing sources is key to conducting historical research. It also provides an important record of your research process. Keeping a "running" bibliography of print and online sources, whether using a program such as *Zotero* or in a word processing document, helps you assess what sources you are using, the balance of primary and secondary materials, and whether or not you need to seek out new kinds of sources to gain a well-rounded perspective on an issue.

Footnotes for a history assignment may vary slightly from those required in other courses. Here are some guidelines to follow for citing various kinds of electronic sources if you do not receive specific instructions in class. The following guidelines are based on the *Chicago Manual of Style*, Fifteenth Edition, and are specific for footnotes or endnotes. For bibliography or reference list styles, visit *The Chicago Manual of Style Online* "Citation Quick Guide," http://www.chicagomanualofstyle.org/tools_citationguide.html.[7]

Website List the author or organization that is responsible for the website, followed by the title of the subsection in quotation marks (if relevant) and the website title in italics, each separated by a comma. Next, list the URL and the date of access in parentheses.

Koninklijke Bibliotheek, National Library of the Netherlands, *Medieval Illuminated Manuscripts*, http://www.kb.nl/kb/manuscripts/ (accessed June 28, 2007).

U.S. Department of State, Office of the Historian, "Kennedy Administration," *Foreign Relations of the United States*, http://www.state.gov/r/pa/ho/frus/kennedyjf/ (accessed July 15, 2007).

Source from an Online Database List the author of the source (if available) followed by the name of the source in quotation marks, name of the database in italics, URL, and date accessed.

Désiré Charnay, "Sentry gate, San Cosme, Mexico City, ca. November 1857–September 1858," *Mexico: From Empire to Revolution*, http://www.getty.edu/research/conducting_research/digitized_collections/mexico/images/7.html (accessed July 10, 2007).

Book Published Electronically List the author(s) of the book, followed by the title, publisher, URL, and date accessed.

Daniel J. Cohen and Roy Rosenzweig, *Digital History: A Guide to Gathering, Preserving, and Presenting the Past on the Web*, University of Pennsylvania Press, http://chnm.gmu.edu/digitalhistory/book.php (accessed June 28, 2007).

Journal Article Published Electronically List the author(s) of the article, article title in quotation marks, journal title and publication information, publisher, URL, and date accessed.

Nara Milanich, "Review Essay: Whither Family History? A Road Map from Latin America," *The American Historical Review* (April 2007), http://www.historycooperative.org/journals/ahr/112.2/milanich.html (accessed June 28, 2007).

Weblog (Blog) Entry or Comment List the author of the entry or comment, followed by identifying information on the entry or comment, name of the blog, date posted, URL, and date accessed.

[7]University of Chicago Press, "Chicago-Style Citation Quick Guide," *The Chicago Manual of Style Online*, 15th ed. (2006), http://www.chicagomanualofstyle.org/tools_citationguide.html (accessed June 28, 2007).

Mills Kelly, entry on "What's It All About?" *Edwired*, entry posted on June 6, 2007, **http://edwired.org/?p=183** (accessed June 28, 2007).

Jonathan Dresner, "Teacher Logic," comment on "History At Play," Rob MacDougall, *CLIOPATRIA: A Group Blog*, comment posted on June 27, 2007, **http://hnn.us/blogs/entries/40294.html** (accessed June 29, 2007).

Email Message List the author of the email, identify it as an email message, include the subject header when possible, and add the date on which it was sent. If the email is personal, note that but do not include the author's email address. Ask permission from the author before citing a personal email message.

Lynn Temple, "Re: Question about the Bedford flag," email message, March 26, 2007.

Listserv Message The format is similar to an email message, but you should include the email address of the listserv.

Liz Ten Dyke, "South Asians in 19th century USA," listserv message, January 17, 2003, **h-world@h-net.msu.edu**.

Using This Guide

This collection of 150 websites is intended as a guide — rather than as an exhaustive list — to finding valuable online resources for exploring world history. The editors selected these websites to illustrate the strengths of the Internet for learning about the past and to demonstrate the incredible range of resources and perspectives available, from electronic texts of Sumerian literature [19] through official documents and diary entries related to the U.S. decision to drop the atomic bomb on Japan [136]. Many excellent websites were not included, but those we have chosen represent some of the best materials available for understanding a broad range of topics and time periods in world history. The emphasis in *World History Matters* is on non-U.S. history websites to complement guides that focus solely on online U.S. history.[8] The U.S. history websites that have been included here address global trends, such as the transatlantic slave trade (*Slaves and the Courts, 1740–1860* [92]), American participation in world events, such as World War I (The Stars and Stripes: *The American Soldiers' Newspaper of World War I, 1918–19* [122]), or large-scale migration or immigration (*Korean American Digital Archive* [112] or *Hispano Music & Culture from the Northern Rio Grande* [111]).

Throughout *World History Matters*, symbols identify the kinds of resources available on each website. ▤ indicates that there are significant written primary sources, such as literary works, official documents, religious texts, letters, or

[8]See *History Matters: A Student Guide to U.S. History Online* (Boston: Bedford/St. Martin's, 2005).

diaries. includes photographs, paintings, drawings, and artifacts. means that audio files, usually music, speeches, or oral history interviews, are available. signifies that a website offers film or video clips, ranging from early film footage to contemporary commercials and interviews. indicates quantitative resources, such as census or price data. identifies the presence of cartographic resources.

The first section, "General Websites for World History Research," introduces resources that cover broad periods of time. Some of these are general, such as *World Art Treasures* [16], with 100,000 images from all time periods and all corners of the world. Others deal with a specific topic or kind of resource across centuries, such as *ArchNet* [2] which emphasizes urban planning and design throughout the Muslim world. The subsequent chapters focus on broad time periods covered in world history survey courses, from the beginnings of human society to the present. We have organized this section into eight chronological groupings. Many websites fall into more than one category, however, and these are cross-referenced at the end of each chronological section (called "More Related Websites").

The Beginnings of Human Society Through 1000 B.C.E.

Classical Traditions, Major Religions, and Giant Empires, 1000 B.C.E.–*300* C.E.

Expanding Zones of Exchange and Encounter, 300–1000 C.E.

Intensified Hemispheric Interactions, 1000–1500

Emergence of the First Global Age, 1450–1770

An Age of Revolutions, 1750–1914

A Half-Century of Crisis and Achievement, 1900–1945

Promises and Paradoxes: The World Since 1945

In the appendix, you will find a glossary of common Internet terms. The index will provide a valuable starting point for locating resources on a specific topic (*e.g.*, "Economy," "Daily Life," "Slavery," "Women"), area of the world (*e.g.*, "Africa" or "North America"), or kinds of primary sources (*e.g.*, "Archaeology," "Maps," "Newspapers"). Types of primary sources are listed in italics; regions are listed in bold. In addition, all of the websites included in this book are listed alphabetically by title on page 113.

— Kelly Schrum and T. Mills Kelly

Key to the Icons

- This website contains written primary sources, such as literary works, official documents, letters, or diaries.
- This website contains images, such as photographs, paintings, drawings, and artifacts.
- This website contains audio files, such as music, speeches, or oral history interviews.
- This website contains film or video clips.
- This website contains quantitative resources, such as census or price data.
- This website contains maps and other cartographic resources.

2

A Selection of Top World History Websites

GENERAL WEBSITES FOR WORLD HISTORY RESEARCH

1. African Voices

Smithsonian, National Museum of Natural History
http://www.mnh.si.edu/africanvoices/

These historical and contemporary images, and accompanying text, provide a survey of African history and culture. Roughly one hundred colorful maps, photographs, drawings, and paintings provide extensive coverage of the continent. Sixteen sections, organized chronologically and thematically, explore Africa's striking diversity and long history by presenting sets of images, a scrollable timeline or set of subthemes, and in some cases, audio and video clips. Material culture is the website's clear strength. Highlights include exhibits on the Makola market in downtown Accra, Ghana, and the tradition of hand dying textiles in Mali. The website provides a general overview of African history and culture as well as richly illustrated nuggets on specific topics in African art. *EAP*

2. ArchNet

MIT School of Architecture and Planning, University of Texas School of Architecture, and Aga Khan Development Network
http://archnet.org/library

This website was created to serve architectural and educational communities interested in urban planning and design throughout the Muslim World. It provides a database of photographic evidence — including thousands of images of historic and contemporary sites — and also presents extensive literary analysis of architecture in Islamic-majority nations. All images are sorted by name, century, usage, style, type, and country, allowing for the study of change and continuity over time in specific regions of the Islamic world. Several galleries explore topics such as the architecture of Ottoman master Sinan, the mud mosques of Mali, pre- and post-war images of Beirut, and Turkey's famous Iznik tiles. Users can make linkages between architecture and other aspects of history and culture in a given society or across societies. Continually updated, *ArchNet*'s collection of photographs of the masterpieces of Islamic architecture may be unrivalled on the Internet, both in terms of scope and accessibility. *NS*

3. Art of Asia

Minneapolis Institute of Arts (MIA)
http://www.artsmia.org/art-of-asia/

The methods that historians use to make sense of material culture come to the fore through this website. Its large collection of art from seventeen Asian cultures is divided by object type and topic, with "Buddhism," "Architecture," and "Ceramics" highlighted on the front page. Japanese items make up the most extensive country-based collection (2,200 pieces), featuring Buddhist objects, traditional interiors, *ukiyo-e* woodblock prints, and architecture. There are close to 1,000 pieces from China accompanied by a "Dynastic Guide" that introduces the varieties of Chinese art production from the Neolithic era (3000–1500 B.C.E.) to the Qing dynasty (1644–1911 B.C.E.). The collection from Korea is smaller, focusing on Korean ceramics dating from the seventh century. A search engine unifies these collections and allows for easy retrieval of specific objects by culture, topic, or type. *MC*

4. Avalon Project: Documents in Law, History, and Diplomacy

Yale Law School

http://www.yale.edu/lawweb/avalon/avalon.htm

This growing collection of more than 600 primary source texts (in translation where necessary) deals with law, history, and diplomacy from the ancient world to the present, with an emphasis on European and U.S. history from the eighteenth through the twenty-first centuries. Documents relating to the Nuremberg War Crimes Trials are extraordinarily rich and include all twenty-two volumes of military court proceeding transcripts. Dozens of supporting texts document Nazi aggression, anti-Jewish propaganda, Adolf Hitler's final orders and testament, and post-war military government in Germany. Other extensive collections include the Federalist Papers, documentation of the Middle East from 1916 to the present, "Nazi-Soviet relations 1939–1941," and official government statements and documents surrounding September 11, 2001. Additional collections (such as "African-Americans: Biography, Autobiography, and History" and groupings of ancient, medieval, and Renaissance documents), however, are smaller and present well-known, frequently cited sources. *JRM*

5. Collect Britain

British Library

http://www.collectbritain.co.uk

More than 90,000 artifacts available through this website highlight some of the British Library's world-renowned collections. The artifacts are organized into nineteen collections, five virtual exhibitions, and three themed tours. Collection topics include historical maps of London streets; plantation life in the Caribbean; the Indian subcontinent; wax cylinder recordings from around the world; Victorian-era sheet music; drawings of English life between 1750 and 1850; the Victorian-era *Penny Illustrated Paper*; Ordnance Survey maps drawn between 1780 and 1840; and watercolors, drawings, and prints from King George III's vast topographical collection. Each collection includes representative images accompanied by bibliographical information and a written description or explanation of the image and its importance. Of special note is the Caribbean Views collection that highlights contrasting depictions of slavery. The "Virtual Exhibitions" section includes sacred manuscripts representing many faiths around the world, drawings and maps that illustrate famous landscapes from English novels, and sketchbooks of the artist Samuel Grimm. *WH*

Stamp from New South Wales, 1850, in *Collect Britain* [5]. *(Copyright © British Library Board. All Rights Reserved. Picture number 1023910.171.)*

6. Digital South Asia Library

American Institute of Indian Studies and Digital South Asia Library, University of Chicago

http://dsal.uchicago.edu/

This extensive website presents a wide range of materials for studying South Asia. The 150,000 high-quality images include mid-nineteenth-century photographs of hill tribes, political life, and architecture, as well as a series of photographs taken by American servicemen during World War II. The image collection is an ideal resource for studying specific geographic locations, daily life, religion, or artistic forms such as sculpture, terracotta, and painting. Additional resources include an extensive collection of statistical information on British colonial India from 1840 to 1920, thirty South Asian language dictionaries, more than twenty-five maps, and bibliographic information. The statistical collection presents scans of documents from British record offices, and is useful for exploring information on economics, demographics, and administrative functions, as well as for considering how and why this kind of information was of value to the British authorities. *RD*

7. EuroDocs

Brigham Young University

http://eudocs.lib.byu.edu/index.php/Main_Page

If you are looking for documents in European history, this website is a good place to begin. It presents thousands of documents generated in forty-six European countries, from Albania to the Vatican City, with the heaviest concentration in British, French, and Scandinavian history. Specific local and family history resources, as well as constitutions and legal documents, are included for these regions. The focus is on "key historical happenings," though the sources encompass a range of political, economic, social, and cultural aspects of European history. The documents date from the Classical Era to the present. This is a mega-site providing links to texts on its own servers as well as elsewhere; thus the accuracy of links cannot be guaranteed. *KDL*

8. Famous Trials

Professor Doug Linder, University of Missouri-Kansas City School of Law

http://www.law.umkc.edu/faculty/projects/FTrials/ftrials.htm

Fifty court trials, from 399 B.C.E. through the present day, are the focus of this website, with extensive primary- and secondary-source materials for each trial. Most of the trials are drawn from U.S. history, but many are relevant for world history. These include: "Trial of Socrates" (399 B.C.E.), "Trial of Jesus" (30 C.E.), "Thomas Moore Trial" (1535), "Trial of Galileo" (1633), "Boston Massacre Trials" (1770), "Mutiny on the Bounty Court Martial" (1792), "Amistad Trials" (1839–1840), "Dakota Conflict Trials" (1862), "Nuremberg Trials" (1945–1949), "The My Lai Courts-Martial" (1970), and the "Moussaoui (9/11) Trial" (2006). Each trial exhibit includes an introductory essay on the historical background of the case, biographies of key figures, and approximately twenty primary documents, including transcripts of testimony, media coverage, depositions, and government documents. Most cases also contain images, links to related websites, and a bibliography of scholarly works. *KDL*

9. Getty Digitized Library Collections

The J. Paul Getty Trust

http://www.getty.edu/research/conducting_research/digitized_collections/

Dedicated to collecting and displaying decorative arts, manuscripts, paintings, drawings, photographs, and sculpture, the Getty presents many items from their collections on this website. "Festivals" highlights prints and drawings from Early Modern European banquets and street fairs. "Irresistible Decay: Ruins Reclaimed" examines European drawings, prints, and photographs of ruins as symbols of continuity and decay. "Monuments of the Future: Designs by El Lissitzky" focuses on a twentieth-

Photograph of the Temples of Hera at Paestum from the *Getty Digitized Library Collections* [9]. *(Permission of Alinari/Art Resource, NY. Image number ART357850.)*

century Russian avant-garde artist. “Study Images of Tapestries” shows photographs of fifteenth-century to eighteenth-century European tapestries. “Early Photography in Greece and the Mediterranean” presents 200 nineteenth-century photographs of sculpture and archaeology from the Classical Era that are invaluable for studying classical Greece, and can also be analyzed as documents of their age — idealized portraits that inspired the neo-classical in the nineteenth century. Additional collections include “A Nation Emerges: Sixty-five Years of Photography in Mexico” and “Prints after Poussin.” Past exhibitions are archived and remain available. *KDL, JC*

10. Huntington Archive of Buddhist and Related Art

Professors John and Susan Huntington, Ohio State University

http://kaladarshan.arts.ohio-state.edu

This searchable database of more than 30,000 black-and-white photographs of art and architecture from Afghanistan, Bangladesh, India, Indonesia, Myanmar (Burma), Nepal, Pakistan, Sri Lanka, and Thailand, includes works of art in their original contexts as well as material located in museums. This vast database is partially contextualized though a “Projects” section — a rather eclectic mix of resources that includes teaching aids, such as maps of Asia and research advice, as well as a noteworthy collection of 1,600 images depicting Newar Buddhist art from Nepal. This section also provides interesting discussions of iconography that will be of great value to those new to these artistic traditions. There are also ten “Online Exhibitions” on topics ranging from Hindu devotional practices and Chinese jade to Japanese basket making and posters from the Cultural Revolution. Any one of these could serve as a short documentary-like introduction to these topics. The images are of exceptional quality and the online viewer features a zoom allowing for the inspection of fine details. *RD*

11. Internet History Sourcebooks Project

Paul Halsall

http://www.fordham.edu/halsall/

A massive amount of source material from ancient through modern history and for most geographic regions of the world is available through this website. Materials are divided into “sourcebooks” — collections of links, divided by subject, to thousands of primary and secondary sources, images, and maps. The resources available here vary as much as the topics they cover. For example, the 104 entries on Egypt in the “Ancient History Sourcebook” include primary sources as well as links to resources on other websites on a range of topics and themes, such as chronologies, historical kingdoms, important figures, religion, art, architecture, literature, music, everyday life, mathematics, gender, and the Black Athena debate. Resources on Islam address Islamic sects, women in Islam, Islamic culture, Crusades, Mongol invasions, ethnic groups such as Turks and Persians, and Islamic expansion into Africa, Asia, and Spain. Other “sourcebooks” are: “Medieval,” “Modern,” “African,” “East Asian,” “Global,” “Indian,” “Jewish,” “History of Science,” “Women,” and “Gay/Lesbian/Bisexual/Trans.” Translations are drawn heavily from the public domain, so more current versions are often available in a library. *KDL*

12. Internet Sacred Text Archive (ISTA)

J.B. Hare

http://www.sacred-texts.com/index.htm

This extensive archive presents sacred texts, throughout history, from many religions and cultural traditions, including Islam, Judaism, Christianity, Buddhism, and Neopaganism. Most texts are in the public domain (published before 1922), providing insight into the thinking and translating process in the late-nineteenth and early-twentieth centuries, as well as the many time periods reflected in the texts. Given advances in linguistics and literary criticism, many translations on the website have been rendered obsolete, and there are almost no references to contemporary scholarship. In addition, there are no obvious criteria at work for identifying a "sacred text." Thus, both *Robin Hood* and the *Rig Veda* are included, as well as texts by Charles Darwin, Mark Twain, and Albert Einstein, among others, that debunk or criticize sacred texts. Nevertheless, the website is relatively easy to navigate and the breadth of the material provided makes it a valuable resource for important documents in world and religious history. JC

13. Kyoto National Museum

Kyoto National Museum

http://www.kyohaku.go.jp/eng/syuzou/index.html

The Kyoto National Museum has one of the most extensive collections of premodern (pre-1800) Asian, and especially Japanese, art in the world. Through this website, it presents 5,000 objects or sets of objects from its English-language catalog. The *Masterworks* section leads to a sampling of more than one hundred of the most significant items in the collection. Items are divided into eight categories: "Archaeology," "Ceramics," "Sculpture," "Paintings," "Calligraphy," "Textiles," "Lacquerware," and "Metalwork." To search the entire collection by category or keyword, select the "On-Line Database" link on the top left corner of the screen. The category search mode provides a useful drop-down list of 150 well-defined options (such as, "Shang/Zhou bronzes" or "Kamakura-era calligraphy"). The one drawback is the lack of commentary accompanying the images. Users could look to Sherman Lee's *History of Far Eastern Art* and Michael Kerrigan's *Asian Art* for a discussion of the themes and methods of Asian art and the historical context for its production. BP

14. LACMA Collections Online

Museum Associates, Los Angeles County Museum of Art

http://collectionsonline.lacma.org/

This website presents more than 70,000 images of artwork and objects from around the world and throughout history and adds new materials regularly. Images are organized by subject — such as "African Art," "Costume and Textiles," and "Prints and Drawings" — which facilitates browsing. A "Quick Tour" option generates random images from all departments to provide a rough sense of the scope of the collection. The most substantial sections are "Japanese Art," with about 2,500 images, and "South and Southeast Asian Art," with 2,000 images. "Photography" offers prints

Painting, *Sailboats on the Seine* by Claude Monet from *LACMA Collections Online* [14]. *(Claude Monet, Sailboats on the Seine, 1874, oil on canvas, 21¼ x 25¾. Permission of Fine Arts Museum of San Francisco, Gift of Bruno and Sadie Adriani, 1962.23.)*

from 1840 to the present. Basic bibliographic data is provided, and most sections include useful historical context and additional background information. All images may be enlarged and manipulated using the Image Viewer, which saves images previously viewed. *KDL*

15. Thinker ImageBase

Fine Arts Museums of San Francisco
http://www.famsf.org/fam/about/imagebase/index.asp

This database contains more than 85,000 images, representing approximately 12,000 artists, that date from the sixth century B.C.E. to the present. Images include paintings, photographs, prints, furniture, pottery, jewelry, functional art, objects, and much more. While most of the images originate from Europe (especially Italy and France), there are more than 1,000 images from other parts of the world. Each image enlarges, can be zoomed for detailed viewing, and is accompanied by basic bibliographic information, including date, artist, title, and medium. However, very little additional content is provided. Users may want to approach this extensive website with historical context and specific search terms in mind as the only browsing options are by country or by century. A useful tool is the "My Gallery" feature (requiring a brief registration process), that allows users to create a personalized art gallery and become virtual curators. *KDL*

16. World Art Treasures

Jacques-Edouard Berger Foundation
http://www.bergerfoundation.ch/

This collection of more than 100,000 images contains paintings, prints, photographs, objects, and architecture from all time periods and all corners of the world, though

Photograph from the Cliff of a Thousand Buddhas, *World Art Treasures* [16]. *(Copyright © Foundation Jacques-Edouard Berger, Lausanne [Sussie].)*

its strength is in European Baroque and Renaissance paintings. La Tour, Vermeer, Botticelli, and Caravaggio are featured prominently, represented by more than one hundred paintings each. The collection is also strong in photographs of East Asian, South Asian, and North African monuments and architecture. The "Lectures and Itineraries" section provides an introduction through images and secondary sources to thirteen subjects, including Rococo, Roman Egypt, Ankor (the capital of the Khmer civilization), and Borobudur (an important Buddhist shrine in Indonesia). The large image library can be browsed by country, artist, or time period, and the website contains a general search function. Many images are available in interactive multimedia format, allowing users to zoom in on small details. *KDL*

WORLD HISTORY WEBSITES BY TIME PERIOD

The Beginnings of Human Society Through 1000 B.C.E.

17. Ancient Mesopotamia: This History, Our History  

University of Chicago Oriental Institute Museum

http://mesopotamia.lib.uchicago.edu/

This website illuminates connections between ancient Mesopotamia and modern Iraq through a collection of sixteen full lesson plans, 142 artifacts, and numerous photographs of archaeological sites. Additional resources include interviews with three archaeologists on the significance of the Code of Hammurabi and the methods museum curators use to preserve and display ancient artifacts. There are detailed analyses of thirteen artifacts, such as children's toys, and fourteen topics surrounding daily life in ancient Mesopotamia, including religion, farming, women's lives, and the invention of writing. A central theme of these materials is the connection between the innovative inventions of Mesopotamians and their essential role in creating key features of civilization still central to our world today. Such linkages provide a history of Iraq that may counter the violent images gleaned from media coverage of the now war-torn nation. *NS*

18. Egypt Archive

Jon Bosworth

http://egyptarchive.co.uk/index.htm

An impressive array of modern photographs of archaeological sites and material culture from ancient Egypt is featured on this website. The majority of the images are of well-known monuments (pyramids, temples, etc.) rather than more work-a-day sites such as the humble but significant "workman's village" of Deir el-Medina from the New Kingdom. The images do not depict commonly photographed views of pyramids, but instead offer admirable, detailed shots of rooms, passageways, architectural oddities, and related material finds. The treatment of the New Kingdom Osireion (precinct of Osiris) at Abydos is particularly useful since it contextualizes detail shots within a view of the larger complex. The lack of context and a search function means that users should be armed with background information before exploring these resources. Nevertheless, the website presents high-quality, detailed photographs from multiple perspectives that allow for close comparison of major Egyptian monuments. *JBL*

Cuneiform school text from *Ancient Mesopotamia* [17]. *(Courtesy of the Oriental Institute of the University of Chicago.)*

19. Electronic Text Corpus of Sumerian Literature

The Oriental Institute, Oxford University

http://www-etcsl.orient.ox.ac.uk

This archive of roughly 400 important texts (transliterations and translations) from ancient Mesopotamia is a focused collection of literary works. It does not contain the standard works from Mesopotamia, such as the *Epic of Gilgamesh* or the *Enuma Elish*, but instead presents lesser-known texts that are more difficult to locate, including early stories about Gilgamesh; poetry in praise of individual monarchs; hymns, prayers, and temple poems; farming instructions; royal correspondence; and poetic documents identified as letters by their use of epistolary formulas. The collection is particularly useful because its focus on a limited cultural and historical context allows for comparisons of religion, kingship, and poetry with better-known Hebrew, Greek, and Indian literatures. For example, comparing the hymns collected here with those in the Biblical Psalms allows users to uncover differences and similarities in cultural and religious outlook between Sumerian and Hebrew cultures. *JBL*

20. Eternal Egypt

Supreme Council of Antiquities, Egyptian Center for Documentation of Cultural and Natural Heritage (CultNat), and IBM

http://www.eternalegypt.org/EternalEgyptWebsiteWeb/HomeServlet

This collection of Egyptian material culture showcases more than 1,500 objects from the last five millennia: items from the Pharaonic era — the main focus of the collection — include familiar artifacts, such as the golden mask of Tutankhamen, which are presented alongside everyday objects, such as a tool commonly used by carpenters (adze). Key resources are also available from the Roman era, the Coptic/Byzantine era, and the Islamic era (for example, the mosque lamp of Sultan Hassan). Sophisticated, yet easy-to-navigate, multimedia presentations allow users to interact virtually with the artifacts and explore connections among them. Supplementary

Illustrated manuscript page from *Eternal Egypt* [20]. *(Supreme Council of Antiquities, Egyptian Center for Documentation of Culture and National Heritage.)*

materials include maps that show important historical and contemporary sites in Egypt and a comprehensive timeline that integrates the artifacts temporally, thus encouraging users to connect artifacts with larger issues in Egyptian history. Additionally, seventy articles explain topics such as women in Egyptian history and daily life on the Nile. *NS*

21. Great Archaeological Sites

French Ministry of Culture and Communication

http://www.culture.gouv.fr:80/culture/arcnat/en/

Fifteen significant archaeological sites or topics ranging from prehistory to the Middle Ages are virtually excavated on this well-designed website. Four topics provide interactive explorations into prehistoric caves: "Cave of Chauvet Pont d'Arc," "Cave of Lascaux," "Cosquer Cave," and "Underwater Archaeology." Each centers on a virtual spelunking tour with fifty enlargeable images of cave paintings and natural archaeological material accompanied by detailed explanations. The project entitled "Gauls in Provence: the *oppidum* at Entremont" provides the opportunity to move between archaeology, archaeological method, and interpretations of cultural contact based on material culture. Through detailed information about interactions between Gallic tribes and Greeks, and the development of settlement (with an eye to Hellenic influences), it shows how Gallic society interacted with Mediterranean neighbors. Other topics include: the Abbey of St. Germaine in Auxerre; a tenth-century agricultural settlement on the shores of Lake Paladru; Ancient Vienne, home of the Allobroges (a warlike Celtic tribe that occupied southeastern France); and the Saqqara site in Egypt. *JBL*

Black varnished ceramics from Campania in *Great Archaeological Sites* [21]. *(French Ministry of Culture and Communication.)*

Photograph of conservation and remodeling from *Mohenjo Daro* [22]. *(Copyright J.M. Kenoyer, Courtesy Dept. of Archaeology and Museums, Govt. of Pakistan.)*

22. Mohenjo Daro 

Dr. Jonathan Mark Kenoyer, University of Wisconsin, Madison

http://www.mohenjodaro.net

This website presents 103 images and supporting secondary-source material from archaeological excavations at Mohenjo Daro, a site in the Indus Valley. The introduction, addressing aspects of this fascinating culture that thrived between 2600 and 1900 B.C.E., presents historical background, major issues, and basic terminology used by archaeologists. The images are divided into categories such as "Indus Plains," "Great Bath," "Drains," "Citadel," "Courtyard," "House," "Street," "Wells," "Boats," "Ancient Villages," "Ringstones," "The Granary," and "Latrines," all of which shed light on aspects of daily life in the ancient Indus culture. Each image is accompanied by a detailed explanation that describes the importance of the specific image and its relation to the site. Taken together, these materials help to teach about the processes by which archaeologists draw conclusions about the past. The website has advertisements and sells books and other products. *RD*

23. Theban Mapping Project   

Theban Mapping Project

http://www.thebanmappingproject.com/

The Valley of the Kings, a burial ground for pharaohs of the New Kingdom in ancient Egypt, is part of ancient Thebes, a royal and priestly enclave that contained palaces, temples, and tombs. This website showcases excavations and discoveries through two interactive atlases of the Valley of the Kings and the Theban Necropolis. An interactive plan allows users to zoom in on various parts of the tombs and offers some short movies and even 3-D access to the tomb site. The sophisticated, interactive visual resources are accompanied by maps and explanatory texts that serve as a springboard to understanding ancient Egyptian history. These resources lend themselves to research on particular tombs, such as the tomb of Tutankhamen, or sites of exceptional pharaohs, as well as beliefs concerning the dead and religion in ancient Egypt. Maps and atlases serve as evidence for discussion of the importance of geography in human settlement. *SAH*

More Related Websites

Diotima: Materials for the Study of Women and Gender in the Ancient World [25]

Harappa: The Indus Valley and the Raj in India and Pakistan [81]

Other Women's Voices: Translations of Women's Writing Before 1700 [47]

Classical Traditions, Major Religions, and Giant Empires, 1000 B.C.E.–300 C.E.

24. APIS: Advanced Papyrological Information System

Columbia University

http://www.columbia.edu/cu/lweb/projects/digital/apis/

As a writing medium, papyrus persisted across a broad span of time, and many societies and languages: from the thirteenth century B.C.E. to the fourteenth century C.E.; from Pharaonic Egypt to the Islamic Caliphate; and from Egyptian hieroglyphics to Persian and Arabic. Due to issues of preservation, though, papyrus documents are recovered nearly exclusively from the desert edges of the Nile Valley. Examples of almost every type of document, from banal lists and contracts to hymns, histories, plays, and poems, survive on papyrus. Many of these are available through this meta-archive containing 18,000 individual documents drawn from universities across the U.S. The University of Michigan collection (**http://www.lib.umich.edu/pap/**) offers "snapshots of daily life" in Egyptian antiquity with correspondence and accounts of individuals, mostly from Hellenistic and Roman Egypt. The *Duke Papyrus Archive* (**http://scriptorium.lib.duke.edu/papyrus/**) groups documents by subject — women

Papyrus of a Christian prayer from *APIS: Advanced Papyrological Information System* [24]. *(Papyrus of a Christian Prayer, Special Collections, Princeton Theological Seminary Libraries.)*

and children, slaves, religion, or food. Examining documents written by women shows that under some circumstances women in Ptolemaic Egypt could own property, engage in contracts, and access the civil judicial system. *JBL*

25. Diotima: Materials for the Study of Women and Gender in the Ancient World

Ross Scaife, Editor in Chief

http://www.stoa.org/diotima/

Women and gender in the ancient Mediterranean are the focus of this extensive collection of materials. Resources include more than sixty current translations of Greek, Latin, Egyptian, and Coptic texts, many with detailed notes, as well as bibliographies and links to additional resources. Selections from Greek and Roman literature include plays, hymns, epigrams, poems, epodes, odes, and satires. Navigating within the sections and texts is very smooth. In *Catullus 16: The Marriage of Peleus and Thetis,* the translator has linked proper names in the poem to a glossary of mythological terms at the bottom of the text. *Antigone* includes an excellent introduction with the complete text of Sophocles' play, enhanced by explanatory footnotes. Also included is *Forty-five Jokes from The Laughter Lover*, the earliest example of a joke book in Western literature. The Egyptian texts, including wills, property disputes, marriage agreements, and inheritance disputes, are an excellent source for understanding social life in ancient Egypt. *RL*

26. LacusCurtius: Into the Roman World

William P. Thayer

http://penelope.uchicago.edu/Thayer/E/Roman/home.html

Users can take a "virtual tour" of many of the major Roman archaeological sites and learn about Roman social life through the materials in this large collection. An array of primary and secondary resources are available, including hundreds of photographs of Roman and Etruscan buildings and monuments (amphitheatres, gates, aqueducts, baths, roads, theatres, tombs), Latin inscriptions, topographical texts, maps, classical dictionaries, topical monographs, links to other Roman websites, and twenty-seven Latin and Greek primary texts with translations. The *Excerpta Valesiana*, Claudian's poetry, and Procopius's *Buildings and Anecdota* provide insight into the late Roman Empire from the reign of Constantine to Justinian. This is also an excellent website for studying historical geography. Most of the chapters from Ptolemy's *Geography* are accompanied by maps and bibliographic notes (including references to the texts of Pliny the Elder and Strabo). Though the website appears disorganized, all texts and images can be searched by keyword. *RL*

27. Perseus Digital Library

Gregory Cane, Editor in Chief

http://www.perseus.tufts.edu

This is the premier website for accessing the literature and archaeology of ancient Greek and Roman culture. The heart of the collection consists of more than 400 primary texts of Greek and Roman literature; indeed, no authors regularly studied are missing. In addition to the works of Classical literature, there is a large anthology of images from museum collections and archaeological sites. The ability to work with both Classical texts and images side-by-side is one of the most useful features. One might, for example, read the *Iliad* and simultaneously view vases that portray episodes from the epic. Finally, *Perseus* offers a suite of tools to help integrate and contextualize primary materials, including an atlas with discussions of important Classical sites, a search tool, and an index. One note of caution: the English translations are often quite old, so you may want to consult more recent translations in your library for in-depth analysis. *JBL*

28. Urban Dharma, Buddhism in America

Rev. Kusala, Thich Tam-Thien
http://www.urbandharma.org/

This Buddhist religious website was designed to introduce contemporary Buddhism to the public. As such, many of its essays are useful for understanding issues surrounding Buddhism's growing popularity in America. For those interested in Buddhism in historical perspective, English translations of close to twenty important early South Asian documents are located in the "Sutra" section. *Sutras* (or *suttas* in the Pali) are condensed versions of longer religious tracts and hold a central place in the Buddhist literary tradition. The translations of the "Turning of the Wheel Sutta" and the "Eightfold Path" can serve as an introduction to early forms of Buddhism and illuminate the importance of Buddhist ideas to the development of South Asian philosophy and ethics. "The Edicts of King Asoka," a collection of royal decrees from the third century B.C.E. Mauryan Dynasty, provide one of the earliest South Asian examples of legal writing and offer valuable access to the policies of this important ruler. *RD*

29. Vindolanda Tablets Online

Center for the Study of Ancient Documents, Oxford University
http://vindolanda.csad.ox.ac.uk/

The Roman auxiliary fortress at Vindolanda behind Hadrian's Wall in Britain has yielded close to 1,000 wooden writing tablets discarded by departing troops. This website offers a complete archive of the tablets whose Latin texts record administrative accounts of the garrison, official reports, and most strikingly, personal letters. While the tablets reflect a relatively brief chronological period (second century C.E.) and geographical area (Northern England), they offer an unparalleled opportunity to examine the processes of historical discovery in the context of multicultural, non-elite Roman society. The men stationed at Vindolanda were Germans writing in Latin who served the Roman army in England and were connected to soldiers living across the Empire. A good place to start is a selection of highlights, including an official account of troop strength, a memorandum on the customs of the Britons, and a letter from one soldier rebuking another for not writing more frequently. Each document is available in Latin transcription and English translation. *JBL*

30. Virtual Catalog of Roman Coins

Professor Robert W. Cape, Jr.

http://artemis.austincollege.edu/acad/cml/rcape/vcrc/

Roman coins illuminate the history, culture, art, and religion of ancient Rome and are also an important source for images of emperors and empresses. This collection of more than 1,200 images of coins contributed by collectors and dealers is searchable by chronology (155 B.C.E.–423 C.E.), iconography, inscription, issuer, and contributor. Alternatively, the Main Catalog allows users to choose coins by date and emperor, listed chronologically, or by a list of families. Choosing a surname ("Julia," for example) locates coins that suggest a family tree and trace a single lineage through generations. Although this website offers only a small, rather haphazard selection of the thousands of Roman coins that were minted, the easy navigation, pictures, and simple text descriptions make this collection a good introduction to numismatics (the study of coins) and a useful supplement to the study of ancient Rome. *JC*

More Related Websites

Ancient Mesopotamia: This History, Our History [17]
Egypt Archive [18]
Eternal Egypt [20]
Getty Digitized Library Collections [9]
Hanover Historical Texts Project [59]
International Dunhuang Project [32]
Kyoto National Museum [13]
Maya Vase Database [33]
Online Medieval and Classical Library (OMACL) [35]
Other Women's Voices: Translations of Women's Writing Before 1700 [47]
PreColumbian Portfolio: An Archive of Photographs [36]
Theban Mapping Project [23]

Expanding Zones of Exchange and Encounter, 300–1000 C.E.

31. Ahlul-Bayt Digital Islamic Library Project

Al-Islam

http://www.al-islam.org/alpha.php

Most websites on Islam are founded by Sunni Muslims. Islam also includes three Shi'ite sects, one of which sponsors this website to present Islamic resources "with particular emphasis on Twelver Shia Islamic school of thought." There are no fun-

Calligraphy of the name of Allah and the Ahlul Kisa from the *Ahlul-Bayt Digital Islamic Library Project* [31]. *(Ahlul-Bayt Digital Islamic Library Project.)*

damental differences over theology between Sunnis and Shi'ites, but Shi'ites believe that the Prophet's family (or *ahlul-bayt*) was especially pious and knowledgeable. Shi'ites have additional prayers and holidays specific to the lives of the Prophet's descendants (or *imams*), and different sources for law. Shi'ites only look to sayings of the Prophet's family and are led by a religious elite, such as the ayatollahs of Iran. Thus many (though not all) of these sources are edited or authored by Iranian ayatollahs, and as such are scholarly and reliable. The hundreds of images and multimedia sources and thousands of full-length primary- and secondary-source texts on this website include important Islamic art, calligraphy, and Shi'ite primary sources in translation. There are 300 photographs and paintings of sacred sites, such as mosques and mausoleums, that can help illustrate diversity in Islamic art and architecture, as well as differences between Islamic and Christian religious monuments. *SAH*

32. International Dunhuang Project

International Dunhuang Project

http://idp.bl.uk

Since the early twentieth century, explorations of the Dunhuang caves and other ancient Silk Road sites have unearthed tens of thousands of paintings, manuscripts, printed documents, and other historical artifacts. This website, with close to 120,000 images of these artifacts — including paintings, textiles, other types of material culture, and many manuscripts — is part of an effort to create one central repository. The manuscripts, written in Chinese, Tibetan, Turkic, Sanskrit, and more than twenty other languages and scripts, reflect the cultural diversity of the enormous geographic area linked together by the ancient Silk Road; they range from Buddhist sutras and Confucian classics to calendars, phrase books, and trade contracts. Most items are not translated (though translations are gradually becoming available), but provide rich visual images. The maps provide a "virtual tour" of the Silk Road by

Vase from *Maya Vase Database* [33].
(Rollout photograph © Justin Kerr, K2668.)

examining the types of manuscripts found at the different sites so users can begin to appreciate the road's "international" flavor. *BP*

33. Maya Vase Database

Foundation for the Advancement of Mesoamerican Studies
http://research.famsi.org/kerrmaya.html

Vases are unique among forms of ancient Maya art in that they typically depict full scenes from life and mythology, including multiple figures in different poses and actions. The vases offer perhaps the most detailed perspective available on courtly life and mythology during the Classic Period (200–900 C.E.). This database presents high-quality rollout photographs of more than 1,400 vases. Walking through the interpretation of just one vase can reveal the difficult but exciting challenge of reconstructing past belief systems. For example, vase 593 shows a group of warriors preparing the sacrifice of a prisoner. The linked article by scholar Elin Danien describes the scene as commemorating the funeral of Lord Muwan, with the sacrifice of Lord Puma from a neighboring city as part of the purification ceremony. Robert J. Sharer's *The Ancient Maya* is a helpful resource when analyzing these vases. *CK*

34. Noble Qur'an

Muslim Student Association
http://cwis.usc.edu/dept/MSA/quran

Sponsored by the Wahhabi Sunni sect (one of four Sunni and three Shi'ite sects in Islam, and the official sect of Saudi Arabia), this website reflects the sect's doctrinal and legal posture, which is fundamentalist, socially conservative, and evangelical in outlook. It is also one of the few websites that provides primary sources related to Islam. The three online translations of the *Qur'an* (or *Koran*) are considered solid and scholarly. One translation dates from the early twentieth century; the other two are more recent. There is little difference in the actual language used in all three, however. The search engine renders the translations especially valuable for study. A search on "women," for example, will reveal the many rights women are guaranteed in Islam's original and most important text. Continuity between the Judeo-Christian and Islamic traditions can also be demonstrated by searching for mention of Biblical figures such as Abraham, Noah, Moses, Mary, and Jesus. Additional resources include a transliteration of the *Qur'an*, introductions to each chapter, and background essays. *SAH*

35. Online Medieval and Classical Library (OMACL)

Douglas B. Killings

http://sunsite.berkeley.edu/OMACL/

Those seeking both representative and unusual pre-modern European texts need look no farther than this online library. The thirty-four texts included here were composed anonymously or by one of fifteen authors ranging chronologically from Hesiod and other post-Homeric, pre-classical Greek writers to Torquato Tasso in the sixteenth century C.E. Icelandic sagas are particularly well represented with eight entire sagas available, from the majestic *Njal's Saga* to less familiar works such as the *Eyrbyggja Saga*. Other genres include epics, Germanic mythology, and romances. The last item is the unusual story of *Barlaam and Ioasaph* (Josaphat), a medieval Christian rendering of the story of the Buddha. This is a good example of cross-cultural influence and transmission in the Middle Ages. Together, these texts also provide the opportunity to examine a variety of genres in medieval literature and to consider why such genres would have been popular among medieval audiences. *JRM*

36. PreColumbian Portfolio: An Archive of Photographs

Foundation for the Advancement of Mesoamerican Studies

http://research.famsi.org/kerrportfolio.html

This database presents quality photographs of more than 2,000 artifacts from pre-Columbian cultures (Maya, Olmec, Zapotec, Aztec) in Central and South America. Ceremonial items and other objects demonstrating a high degree of artistic fashioning are included, though objects for everyday domestic use are not. The most noteworthy photographs include the Yaxchilan Lintels (which depict male and female rulers ritually spilling their own blood in order to receive a vision from a divine ancestor), and the famous stone image of Coyolxauhqui, depicting her mythological decapitation at the hand of her brother, Huitzilopochtli, the patron god of the Aztecs. The website includes a mummy bundle and three mummy masks from Peru, which could be part of an investigation into ancient beliefs about death and the afterlife. These materials are also useful for examining pre-Columbian culture more generally. Users might select one iconographic element (such as the moon, rabbit, dog, jaguar, or peccary), or choose one cultural element (such as the ballgame, sacrifice, childbirth, the calendar, hieroglyphic writing, or the roles of women) to investigate. *CK*

More Related Websites

APIS: Advanced Papyrological Information System [24]

Christian Classics Ethereal Library [55]

Epistolae: Medieval Women's Latin Letters [39]

Eternal Egypt [20]

Great Archaeological Sites [21]

Kyoto National Museum [13]
LacusCurtius: Into the Roman World [26]
Medieval Illuminated Manuscripts [46]
Other Women's Voices: Translations of Women's Writing Before 1700 [47]
Perseus Digital Library [27]
Topkapi Museum [65]

Intensified Hemispheric Interactions, 1000–1500 C.E.

37. Amiens Cathedral

Visual Media Center, Columbia University
http://www.learn.columbia.edu/Mcahweb/Amiens.html

Amiens cathedral is one of the most splendid Gothic structures of medieval France. This website offers a virtual tour of the entire cathedral interior through a collection of forty QuickTime movies. Clicking on dots on the cathedral ground plan, found on the menu on the left-hand side of the webpage, allows for full 360-degree views from throughout the cathedral. Also included are twenty-six captioned photographs that convey a sense of movement through different locations; fourteen attractive computer-designed still views of cathedral spaces; sixteen older diagrams, sketches, elevations, and plans of both the cathedral and town of Amiens; and a collection of approximately ninety-five exterior and 125 interior photographs. Ground plan diagrams for the interior helpfully identify the angle of the viewer's perspective. Despite rough spots (a defunct discussion board, poor navigation), this website offers an excellent opportunity to practice matching images in photographs to their location on an architectural ground plan. *JRM*

38. De Re Militari: Online Resources for Medieval Warfare

Society for Medieval Military History
http://www.deremilitari.org/resources/resources1.htm

This broad portal presents materials on the technical, tactical, social, economic, political, religious, diplomatic, geographic, and gendered aspects of war from the late Roman Empire (fifth century C.E.) through the seventeenth century C.E. War is broadly defined as any armed conflict, even between individuals in a feud. More than 400 primary sources and 400 secondary-source articles are hosted both on and off this website. Texts are arranged by region, covering areas from Iceland to Japan, and by subject, covering topics from the Imperial Romans to the Crusade of the Imperial Holy Alliance in the early seventeenth century. Some entire texts are provided (especially about the Crusades), but most of the selections are extended excerpts, for example, from the "Song of Roland" (early twelfth century) or Froissart's "Chronicles" of the Hundred Years' War (through 1400 C.E.). *CG*

39. Epistolae: Medieval Women's Latin Letters

Joan Ferrante, Columbia University, and Columbia Center for New Media, Teaching, and Learning

http://epistolae.ccnmtl.columbia.edu/

The religious, economic, and political lives of powerful women in medieval Europe are revealed through this collection of their letters, written between the fourth and thirteenth centuries. More than eighty women — including well-known correspondents, such as Heloise and Abelard, and lesser-known authors — are included. The letters help address the popular misperception of the medieval period as a static era by shedding light on the changes in women's lives across time. The Christian Church's concerns about women's spiritual practices are visible in the correspondence of the early-fifth-century Roman noble woman, Principia, the eighth-century British abbess, Bugga, and thirteenth-century Clare of Assisi. The correspondence of the eleventh-century Empress Agnes of Poitiers and the formidable Eleanor of Aquitaine reveal first-hand the diplomatic and financial power they wielded, combating the notion that women exercised power exclusively in the domestic sphere. Historical notes and biographical sketches accompany each letter, rendering them, and the themes they address, accessible to non-specialists. *NJ*

40. Florence Catasto of 1427

Professor R. Burr Litchfield, Brown University

http://www.stg.brown.edu/projects/catasto/overview.html

Faced with protracted warfare against the duchy of Milan, the leaders of the Florentine Republic declared a new tax survey — *Catasto* — for all citizens of Florence in May 1427. Officials visited and interviewed every head of household in the city, a total of 9,780 individuals. Nearly twenty different variables were recorded, including occupation, age, marital status, number of mouths to feed, debts, property holdings, domestic animals owned, and tax assessment. All of the information is available through this searchable database. Users can analyze the city of Florence as a social community and identify elite or non-elite families, or can search the *Catasto* for individual names, where it becomes apparent that wealthier families tended to have more independent heads of household in Florence than poorer ones. In turn, this information provides a rare detailed glimpse into the urban landscape and family life of Renaissance Florence. *MPH*

41. Florilegium Urbanum

Stephen Alsford

http://www.trytel.com/~tristan/towns/florilegium/flor00.html

Inspired by the medieval concept of a textual anthology illuminating specific topics, this website allows users to explore more than 200 short primary sources and excerpts from longer texts dealing with medieval English towns. Each translated source is accompanied by original edition information and a discussion of historical context. The Introduction presents views of English towns from several medieval perspectives. Two are descriptions of London that date to the twelfth century: an unfavorable account of city life composed by a Winchester monk, and a more optimistic view by Thomas Becket's biographer. The remaining sections deal respectively with four aspects of town life: community, economy, government, and lifecycle. Each of these is divided into subsections framed by substantial introductory essays. This website is useful beyond its function as a document database, as it is part of the larger Medieval English Towns website that contains individual town sources, biographical sketches for citizens of Lynn, and a glossary. *JRM*

42. Index of Medieval Medical Images

UCLA Digital Library

http://digital.library.ucla.edu/immi/

Drawn from manuscripts created between 1250 and 1500, this site presents more than 500 images pertinent to medicine in the Middle Ages, including scalpels, medicinal plants, surgical techniques, and diagnostic charts for such things as alcoholism and physical abnormalities. The images are high-quality and are usually displayed as part of the entire manuscript page in which they appeared, showing how the image might have been incorporated into the surrounding text. Image pages are also accompanied by information about the date, provenance, topic(s), and physical characteristics of the manuscript, as well as a brief discussion of what the image depicts. This website offers a way to explore a pre-professional medieval medical world that valued the restorative qualities of nature, but that also embarked on scientifically informed studies of illness, anatomy, and surgeries. Drawn from materials held in North American libraries, these resources can be used to study the history of science and medicine, especially themes of interfaith and cross-cultural exchange. *CG*

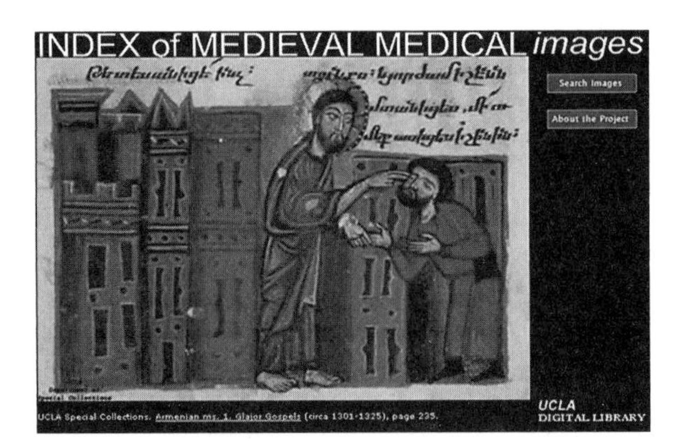

Screenshot from *Index of Medieval Medical Images* [42]. *(The Cure of the Blind Man at Bethsaida, by T'oros T'aronec'i. Armenian Ms. 1, Gladzor Gospels. Department of Special Collections, Charles E. Young Research Library, UCLA.)*

43. Mapping Margery Kempe: A Guide to Late Medieval Material and Spiritual Life

Sarah Stanbury and Virginia Raguin, College of the Holy Cross

http://www.holycross.edu/departments/visarts/projects/kempe/

Margery Kempe, a woman who desired to live a spiritual life in the early fifteenth century, composed what is often recognized as the first English autobiography, *The Book of Margery Kempe*, in 1438. In her spiritual journal, dictated to a scribe, Kempe describes her mystical visions, spiritual travels, and impressions of secular life. She also details the trials she faced as a mystic whose authenticity was doubted by her peers and clerical supervisors. This collection of resources examines the social context in which Kempe produced her narrative and provides a complete transcription of the autobiography in English along with ample secondary material, including lengthy biographical introductions to Kempe and a substantial glossary of terms, places, and people mentioned in her writings. Hundreds of images and photographs, found in the *Parish and Cathedral* section, include related parishes, cathedrals, and devotional images. *NJ*

44. Matrix

Lisa M. Bitel, University of Southern California, and Katherine Gill, Hill Monastic Manuscript Library

http://monasticmatrix.usc.edu/

This database has a clear mission statement: "to document the participation of Christian women in the religion and society of medieval Europe . . . [and] to collect and make available all existing data about all professional Christian women in Europe between 400 and 1600 C.E." To that end, it includes a collection of thousands of profiles of all women's religious communities in medieval Europe (*Monasticon*), forty-five primary source texts (*Cartularium*), close to 1,000 secondary source texts (*Commentaria*), and biographical profiles of 600 religious women (*Vitae*). The website also provides 300 images of architecture, sculpture, book illuminations (*Figurae*), and a bibliographical catalog of works on medieval women, including more than 1,100 primary sources and 4,000 secondary sources (*Bibliographia*). These vast resources are useful for many different types of projects. For example, those wishing to compare female religious communities of the same order in different countries can use the *Monasticon* search engine to find all community profiles for, say, Dominican houses in France, Germany, and Italy (searching one region at a time). *JRM*

45. Medieval and Early Modern Data Bank

Rutgers University, Research Libraries Group, Inc.

http://www2.scc.rutgers.edu/memdb/

This website provides access to five sets of data on European currency exchange and commodities prices from the thirteenth through the eighteenth centuries dealing

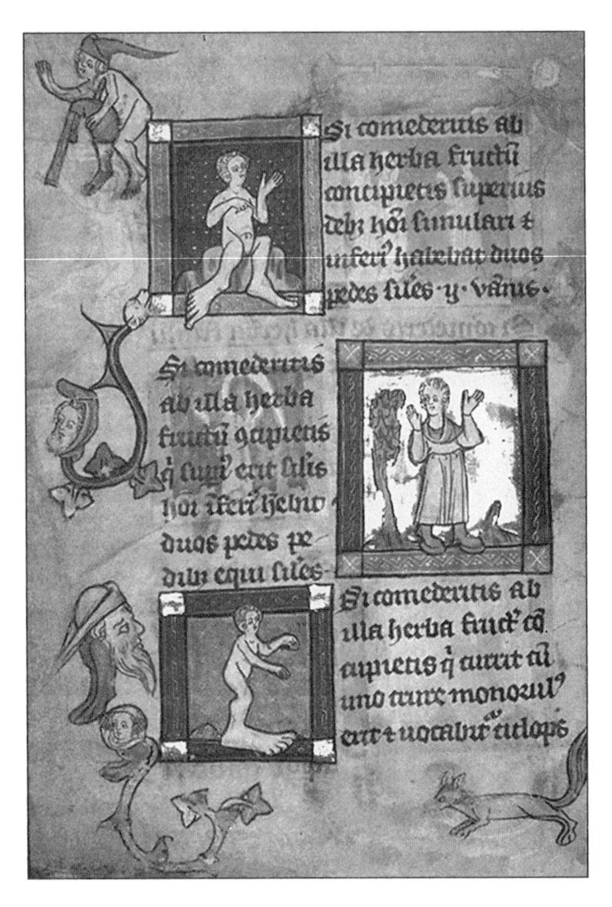

Page from the Rothschild Canticles in *Matrix* [44]. *(Courtesy of the Beinecke Rare Book and Manuscript Library, Yale University.)*

chiefly with the Rhineland, the Low Countries, and Venice. Three of the sets provide data on currency exchanges and two sets cover prices for grain and other commodities in Cologne and Amsterdam. With every search, a results page displays a table and allows results to be exported to a file readable by Excel-compatible spreadsheet programs, allowing users to manipulate the data. For example, to examine the possible effect of the Thirty Years' War (1618–1648) on the consumption and prices of grain using the Prices (Metz) database, run queries on oats and wheat sales and prices in Cologne for the period 1600–1650. After importing this data into a spreadsheet, it is possible to create a comparative sheet and graph that display a dramatic downturn in wheat and oats sales, though not prices, from the 1620s through the 1640s. Those studying the drop in German population during the Thirty Years' War would be able to draw tentative conclusions from such data, namely that demand for grain tapered off dramatically as a result of depopulation. *JRM*

46. Medieval Illuminated Manuscripts

Koninklijke Bibliotheek, National Library of the Netherlands

http://www.kb.nl/manuscripts/

This collection of 11,000 manuscript illuminations (miniatures, initials, and border decorations) is drawn from close to 400 manuscripts, primarily late medieval manuscripts from France and the Low Countries. The "Highlights" section is an attractive starting point for users who want to learn about themes for specialized searches, such as church and society, Christian holidays, the Bible, and topics like "fabulous animals" or "devils and demons." The "Browse by Subject" feature is especially useful for thematic comparisons and stylistic or compositional change over time. For example, a fourteenth-century *Majestas Domini* image from Amiens looks quite different from one in a set of gospels from Tournai dating to roughly 900. Daily life in the Middle Ages can be glimpsed by browsing "eating and drinking," which yields twenty-eight manuscript images of scenes depicting the marriage feast at Cana or Esau's sale of his birthright in return for a bowl of lentils. *JRM*

47. Other Women's Voices: Translations of Women's Writing Before 1700

Dorothy Disse

http://home.infionline.net/~ddisse/

This collection of more than 125 texts written by women spans from 2300 B.C.E. to the early eighteenth century C.E., and from the Middle East to Asia to Europe. The

Folio from *Suffrage to St. Agatha of Catania* from *Medieval Illuminated Manuscripts* [46]. *(Courtesy of the Koninklijke Bibliotheek, The Netherlands.)*

majority of the women represented were nobility, but writings from other women are also presented here. Examples include the works of Sei Shonagon, a prominent literary figure and attendant at the Japanese court in the tenth century, and Rabi'a al-'Adawiyya, of Basra, Iraq, who may have been a freed slave living in the 700s. Available texts include drama, prose, poetry, biography, visionary literature, history, memoirs, and letters that shed light on how women viewed such diverse topics as war, crime, class, sexuality and sex roles, and especially religion in the particular contexts in which they lived. The website offers a biographical portrait of each writer with pertinent facts, but not much historical context. Thus, users may want to approach this website armed with a good world history textbook. *NJ*

48. Scrolls of the Mongol Invasion of Japan

Bowdoin University, Educational Research and Development Program

http://www.bowdoin.edu/mongol-scrolls/

In the thirteenth century, Takezaki Suenaga, a Japanese warrior who fought against the Mongols, commissioned a set of scrolls depicting the Mongol invasions. The scrolls disappeared, but were rediscovered in the eighteenth century. This website includes four versions of the scrolls: the original thirteenth-century scroll, eighteenth- and nineteenth-century reconstructions, and a twenty-first-century restoration of the original. Users examine the scrolls from right to left in one continuous motion either individually or two at a time in a split screen that allows for side-by-side comparison. Detailed zoom views allow those interested in studying the details of Japanese armor and weaponry — or those interested in the visual representation of severed Mongol heads — to spend hours exploring the rich imagery. Though the website is not intended to provide an encyclopedic introduction to the Mongol invasions of Japan, it provides an important visual resource as well as a compelling inside look into the kinds of sources that historians use when writing about the past. *BP*

49. TEAMS Middle English Texts

Medieval Institute Publications

http://www.lib.rochester.edu/camelot/teams/tmsmenu.htm

This well-organized, academically rigorous website offers a portal into the world of medieval English literature through more than 350 texts, including poems, prose narratives, sermons, guidelines for nuns, and marital advice. Reflecting surviving material, the writings are heavily biased toward the thirteenth through fifteenth centuries, although there are samples of Old English texts (through the Norman Conquest of 1066) and Middle English texts (through Shakespeare). Most texts are related to those most commonly examined from this era. Thus, while the popular *Beowulf*, *Piers the Plowman*, and *Canterbury Tales* are absent, the collection does include "The Canterbury Interlude" and "The Merchant's Tale of Beryn," both anonymous fifteenth-century additions to Geoffrey Chaucer's *Tales* that explained the pilgrims' arrival in Canterbury. Each text is accompanied by a scholarly introduction to the cultural background of the topics and texts, a synopsis of the text(s), and a discussion of surviving manuscripts. These writings introduce the breadth of topics (lay and religious) and styles (bawdy and spiritual) covered in the earliest examples of English vernacular texts. *CG*

More Related Websites

American Journeys [51]
Atlantic Slave Trade and Slave Life in the Americas: A Visual Record [52]
British History Online [54]
Christian Classics Ethereal Library [55]
From History to Herstory: Yorkshire Women's Lives Online, 1100 to the Present [79]
Hanover Historical Texts Project [59]
International Dunhuang Project [32]
Kyoto National Museum [13]
Online Medieval and Classical Library (OMACL) [35]
PreColumbian Portfolio: An Archive of Photographs [36]
Topkapi Museum [65]

Emergence of the First Global Age, 1450–1770

50. Afriterra, The Cartographic Free Library

Afriterra Foundation Library
http://www.afriterra.org/

A quick glance at the more than 1,000 maps of Africa presented here reveals an important lesson: European mapmakers did not know much about Africa. These maps were created between the late fifteenth century and the twentieth century, with most originating in the sixteenth, seventeenth, and eighteenth centuries. They are very accessible and users can easily pan, zoom in and out, and track the position of the zoom within the whole image. Even when viewed at great magnification, the images retain high resolution and clarity. Highlights include Berlinghieri's 1482 maps of northwest Africa as well as Forlani's 1566 map, which shows that European explorers were frequently in the dark regarding even basic information, such as the relative proportions of the continent. The maps can be used to explore many topics, including African history, Atlantic World history, the slave trade, the era of European expansion, environmental history, and military history. *EAP*

51. American Journeys

Wisconsin Historical Society
http://www.americanjourneys.org

The words of explorers, Native Americans, traders, missionaries, and settlers come to life through this collection of more than 180 texts describing encounters with North America. The collection ranges widely in scope and date, including works by early Viking explorers in Canada through journals of nineteenth-century American explorers. Though the focus is on North American history, British, French, and

Spanish explorers are featured, notably the journals and letters of Christopher Columbus, several works by Jacques Cartier, and five letters and accounts by Spanish explorer Juan de Oñate. A good place to begin is the "Highlights" section, which provides links to texts documenting important events in North American history — for example, Pocahontas's rescue of John Smith, and Jacques Marquette and Louis Jolliet's arrival at the Mississippi from Canada. All documents are provided in English translation and can be easily downloaded and printed. In addition, more than 750 drawings, maps, photographs, and paintings provide historical context. *KDL*

52. Atlantic Slave Trade and Slave Life in the Americas: A Visual Record

Jerome S. Handler, Virginia Foundation for the Humanities and Michael L. Tuite, Jr.
http://hitchcock.itc.virginia.edu/Slavery/index.php

These 1,000 images depict Atlantic slavery, encouraging viewers to see slavery as a pan-Atlantic system rather than a phenomenon limited to one region. Images are divided into categories, including "Maps," "New World Agriculture and Plantation Labor," "Music, Dance, and Recreational Activities," and "Military Activities." The smallest categories have nine images each ("Family Life, Child Care, Schools" and "Emancipation and Post-Slavery Life") while the largest category has 180 ("Pre-Colonial Africa"). Most of the images are from the seventeenth through nineteenth centuries, although there are some recent images, such as twentieth-century sculptures from Haiti and Barbados. Images include engravings, paintings of events and people, and photographs of slave forts and artifacts, such as ritual objects and punishment devices. In showcasing the social, political, economic, and cultural practices of Africans and their descendants on both sides of the Atlantic, the images provide a broad view of people's lives rather than defining them by their labor and status as slaves. *JB*

Picture of slaves conversing from *Atlantic Slave Trade and Slave Life in the Americas* [52]. *(Courtesy of the John Carter Brown Library at Brown University.)*

53. Bodleian Library Broadside Ballads

Bodleian Library, University of Oxford

http://www.bodley.ox.ac.uk/ballads/ballads.htm

Broadside ballads were popular songs that were printed, frequently with lavish woodcut illustrations, and sold at relatively affordable prices in Britain between the

A Halter for *Rebels* :

O R,

The *Jacobites* Downfall.

A Moſt Excellent New Ballad to a merry Old Tune, Call'd --- *The Old Wiſe ſhe ſent to the Miller her Daughter.*

I.

A Junᶜto of Knaves met at *Paris* together,
Leud *St. John*, Bloody *Berwick*, and ſeveral more,
With *Frenchify'd Ormond*, all Birds of a Feather,
Declaring for *Perkin*, that Son of a Whore ;
Each ſmil'd and embrac'd, Opinions expreſt,
And their Loyalty thus to young *Jemmy* confeſt ;
They ſwore the Lov'd *Shamſter* to *Britain* they'd bring,
And all the Day long,
This, this was their Song,
Dear Jemmy, *Dear* Jemmy, *depend on't, thou ſhalt be a King.*

II.

Tho' *Marlborough*'s with *GEORGE*, Sirs, tho' we are diſbanded,
Tho' our Plots are diſcover'd, our Old Schemes undone,
If once more we get but our dear Hero landed,
Great Britain ſhall yet be a Province of *Rome* ;
Of the Church's great Danger we'll loudly complain,
Fool the Mob to believe it, or all is in vain;
They ſwore the Lov'd Shamſter to *Britain* they'd bring,
And all the Day long,
This, this was their Song,
Dear Jemmy, *Dear* Jemmy, *depend on't, thou ſhalt be a King.*

III.

But e're this Vile Treaſon was brought to Concluſion,
The *Senate* the *Jacobite* Rogues did detect,
Great *GEORGE* rais'd his Troops to their Utter Confuſion,
Reſolv'd our *Religion* and *Laws* to protect ;
E'ry Day ſome New Rebel to *Bar le* takes Poſt,
Whilſt *Bob* in the Cage ſwears the Game is all loſt ;
In vain they cry help us, Oh ! *Lewis* and *Rome,*
And all the Day long,
Now this is their Song,
Dear Jemmy, *an Halter, an Halter's our Doom.*

LONDON Printed, and Sold by *A. Boulter* without *Temple-Bar* 1715

Folio from "A Halter for Rebels" in *Bodleian Library Broadside Ballads* [53]. *(Bodleian Library, University of Oxford, Harding B3(67), printed by A. Boulter.)*

sixteenth and eighteenth centuries. The ballads celebrated contemporary events and figures and were an early means of mass communication. Today they serve as an invaluable resource for studying British cultural and social history as well as the history of printing. This collection of more than 30,000 songsheets is perhaps the largest in the U.K. The Some Images section provides a useful introduction, illustrating how one song was tailored for local markets. The browse/search function allows users to find ballads dealing with specific topics, and explore popular attitudes. Many broadsides contain only words and a reference to a popular tune to which the new song would be sung. Thirteen sound files offer examples of such popular tunes. *WH*

54. British History Online

Institute of Historical Research and the History of Parliament Trust
http://www.british-history.ac.uk/

Thousands of documents pertaining to the legal, political, intellectual, cultural, urban, local, and religious histories of the British Isles are gathered here, serving as a formidable introduction to British history in the eleventh through nineteenth centuries. They include material relating to churches and religious houses, commerce, trade, taxation, population and property, topography and ordnance surveys, architectural studies, debating societies, and physicians practicing in London. The collection is particularly strong in the sixteenth and seventeenth centuries, and in the London and South East regions. Notably present is the full text of the parliamentary debates held between 1667 and 1694. These verbatim records of a vital period in the establishment of the constitutional monarchy provide a wealth of information on legal and fiscal policies. The full-text search feature is especially useful for unearthing topics that are not included in the subject headings, such as women and children. *PL*

55. Christian Classics Ethereal Library

Calvin College
http://www.ccel.org

Created by a Christian college with the goal of "build[ing] up the church by making classic Christian writings available and promoting their use," this website addresses all aspects of the history of Christianity with more than 850 English-language texts. It is especially strong in the areas of the church fathers, from Augustine through Aquinas, as well as the Reformations of the sixteenth and seventeenth centuries. There are versions of the Bible and the Psalms, copious correspondence, creeds, catechisms, hymns, and liturgies. There are also many literary classics, including the full text of Dante's *Divine Comedy*. Some of the longer texts are rendered more useful online than in print form due to the advanced search feature. Users can quickly find examples of how Augustine and John Calvin used terms like *grace* or *predestination*, or what they had to say about sex and marriage. Although there are few writings from the secondary reformers such as Philip Melancthon, Theodore Beza, and Martin Bucer, this collection is quite easily the best single online location for source materials in English for the Reformation period. *MPH*

56. Complete Works of William Shakespeare

Jeremy Hylton

http://shakespeare.mit.edu/works.html

Among the bewildering variety of Shakespeare websites, this one stands out as particularly user-friendly. It offers the complete Shakespeare plays — comedies, histories, and tragedies — with clear, readable text and a scroll option. The source for the plays, the Moby Shakespeare, is no longer available online, which makes complete citation somewhat problematic. Nevertheless, the website is straightforward, a model of good design and organization. To augment Shakespeare's language with related images, *Illustrated Shakespeare* (**http://digital.library.wisc.edu/1711.dl/IllusShake**) examines how artists and book publishers responded to Shakespeare's works, allowing users to consider why certain scenes were selected for illustration, and how nineteenth-century artists chose to depict those scenes. These plays were intended to be spoken and acted, so find a friend and read aloud or act out these plays to fully immerse yourself in the language of Shakespeare. *MH*

57. Galileo Project

Professor Albert Van Helden, Rice University

http://physics.ship.edu/~mrc/pfs/110/inside_out/vu1/Galileo/index-2.html

Galileo Galilei, an Italian scientist and mathematician, is a key figure in the scientific revolution of seventeenth-century Europe. This website, devoted to Galileo's life and work, presents personal and professional resources. An extensive timeline provides more than fifty illustrations — many created by Galileo himself — and information on all of Galileo's major scientific ideas, such as motion, sunspots, the telescope, and the moons of Jupiter. A tour through "Galileo's Villa" provides information on Galileo's family, a seminar on Galileo's experiments in physics and mechanics, images of seventeenth-century scientists and churchmen, and information about the Inquisition. Between 1623 and 1634, Galileo Galilei's daughter (a Franciscan nun) wrote him more than 120 letters, which present a unique view into the mind of one of the giants of the Scientific Revolution through the words of his daughter. These letters also contain information on Galileo's family life, and provide a running commentary on Galileo's efforts to publish his revolutionary scientific findings without attracting the ire of the church. *MPH*

58. Guamán Poma: *El primer nueva corónica y buen gobierno*

Royal Library of Denmark

http://www.kb.dk/permalink/2006/poma/info/en/frontpage.htm

In 1615, native Andean Felipe Guamán Poma de Ayala completed his *Nueva corónica y buen gobierno,* or *New Chronicle and Good Government,* to provide the Spanish king with an Andean perspective on colonial Peru. This website offers an introductory essay and presents images of the manuscript's 1,200 pages, including close to 400 drawings. Guamán Poma wrote about pre-conquest Andean history and also described what he saw as the damaging effects of Spanish colonization on indigenous society. His images of European and Inca rulers and scenes of Inca and

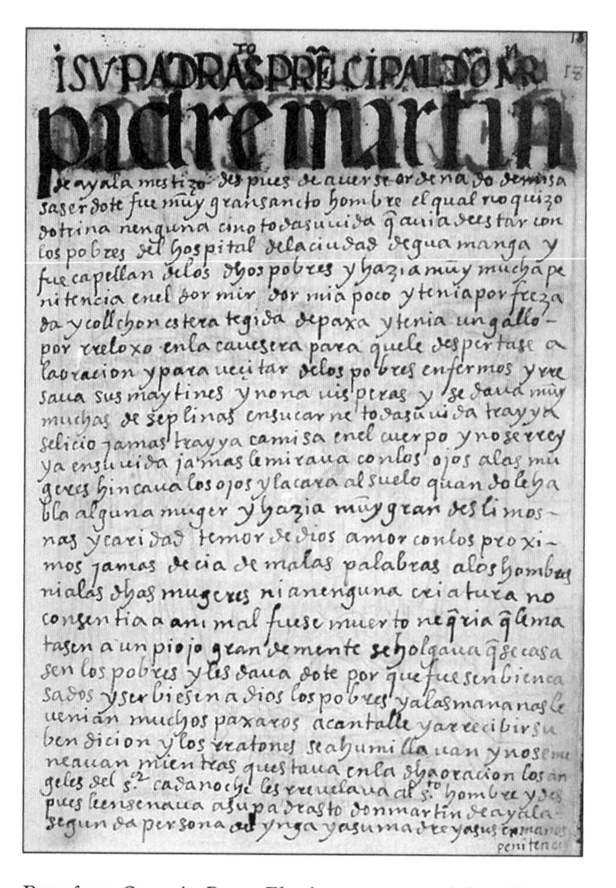
SU PADRASPRĒCIPAL DON

padre martin

de ayala mestizo despues de auerse ordenado de misa
saserdote fue muy gran santo hombre el qual no quizo
dotrina ninguna cino toda su uida q auia de estar con
los pobres del hospital de la ciudad de guamanga y
fue capellan de los dhos pobres y hazia muy mucha pe
nitencia en el dormir dormia poco y tenia por freza
da y colchon estera tegida de paxa y tenia un gallo -
por reloxo en la cauesera para que le despertase a
la oracion y para ueçitar de los pobres enfermos y re
zaua sus maytines y nona uisperas y se daua muy
muchas de seplinas en su carne toda su uida traya ci
selicio jamas traya camisa en el cuerpo y no se rrey
ya en su uida jamas le miraua con los ojos a las mu
geres hincaua los ojos y la cara al suelo quando le ha
bla alguna muger y hazia muy gran des li mos -
nas y caridad temor de dios amor con los proxi -
mos jamas decia de malas palabras a los hombres
ni a las dhas mugeres ni a ninguna criatura no
consentia a animal fuese muerto ne q ria q llma
tasen a un piojo gran demente se holgaua q se casa
sen los pobres y les daua dote por que fuesen bienca
sados y seruiesen a dios los pobres y alas mananas le
uenian muchos paxaros a cantalle y a rrecibir su
bendicion y los rratones se ahumillauan y no se me
neauan mientras questaua en la dha oracion los an
geles del s.^r cada noche les rreuelaua al s.^to hombre y des
pues le ensenaua a su padrasto don martin de ayala -
segunda persona del ynga y asu madre y asus ermanos
penitencia

Page from *Guamán Poma*: El primer nueva corónica y buen gobierno [58]. *(Felipe Guamán Poma de Ayala, Nueva corónica y buen gobierno (1615). Ms. GKS 2232 4to, p. 18. Courtesy of The Royal Library, Copenhagen.)*

colonial life show the diversity of people in the colony, including European priests and royal officials, indigenous nobles and workers, and African slaves. The images also depict Spanish abuses of indigenous people through overwork and punishment. Comparing this manuscript with excerpts of Spanish accounts, such as Pedro de Cieza de León's *The Discovery and Conquest of Peru*, provides the opportunity to think about the relationship between events and how they are recorded. JB

59. Hanover Historical Texts Project

Hanover University

http://history.hanover.edu/project.html

This collection features more than 115 primary source texts in English focusing mainly on European history, with a few resources on Ancient Greece and Rome, the United States, Africa, and Asia. Some categories have only one or two readings, while others, such as Early Modern Europe, are more complete. This site features a solid collection of documents pertaining to Tudor and Stuart England, and particularly to issues of religion and the Crown. There is also material on France under Louis XIV, Martin Luther and religion, witches and witchcraft (but nothing on the Inquisition that tried witches in Catholic countries), and the Italian Renaissance, though documents on Spain are notably absent. The "best of site" award, though, goes to Lorenzo Valla's work on the "Donation of Constantine," which is paired with a bilingual copy of the original "Donation," taken from Gratian's *Decretum*. Valla's essay is a model of critical reading, and can serve as an introduction to that style of writing. *MH*

60. Historic Cities: Maps and Documents

Department of Geography at the Hebrew University of Jerusalem and the Jewish National and University Library

http://historic-cities.huji.ac.il/historic_cities.html

Maps of 170 cities — from Aden to Zurich and many cities in between — created between the fifteenth and eighteenth centuries are featured on this website. Most of the cities are in Eastern and Western Europe, the Mediterranean world, and the Middle East. There are more than 300 maps of Jerusalem alone. In addition, fifteen cities in northern and southern Africa are represented, as are Mexico City; Cuzco (Cusco), Peru; and several cities in India. Each map is accompanied by information about the city, such as geographic location and political importance, date, cartographer, and publication information. The website also includes biographies of close to thirty European mapmakers, including editor Georg Braun and engraver Franz Hogenberg whose *Civitates orbis terrarum* is the source for many of the maps. This level of contextualization provides the opportunity for interesting comparisons across time and space, tracing the development of one mapmaker, perhaps, or views of a specific city over time. *KDL*

Drawing of Bari, Italy, in *Il Regno di Napoli* from *Historic Cities* [60]. *(The Jewish National & University Library, Shapell Family Digitization Project and The Hebrew University of Jerusalem, Dept. of Geography, Historic Cities Project.)*

61. Medici Archive Project

Medici Archive Project
http://www.medici.org

Established by Grand Duke Cosimo I in 1569, this extensive archive of the Medici Grand Dukes documents political and courtly life in Renaissance and Baroque Europe. Containing nearly three million letters, the archive sheds light on courtly life, war, diplomacy, and especially the running of a Renaissance or Baroque state. One third of the archive consists of diplomatic correspondence. The database presents documents that have been cataloged and are searchable by word, topic, place, date, and person. Each record contains a passage of about 250 words in the original Tuscan (the forerunner of modern Italian), as well as a summary of the document in English. Additional sections on topics as diverse as "Jewish History" and "Costumes and Textiles" highlight important content in the archive. *MPH*

62. Proceedings of the Old Bailey

The Old Bailey Proceedings Online
http://www.oldbaileyonline.org

Examining the "Old Bailey" — the popular name for London's main criminal court until 1834 when it became the Central Criminal Court — provides an enormous window onto the history of crimes and misdemeanors in London from the seventeenth to the nineteenth centuries. This website presents a collection of records from 100,000 criminal trials, ranging from theft to sexual crimes to murder, transcribed from the court's official record book, the *Proceedings of the Old Bailey.* Over the 150 years this website covers, the *Proceedings* evolved from a popular publication emphasizing sensationalist crimes, particularly sexual offenses, into a quasi-official account of the court's trials for the benefit of legal professionals. The search and browse features lend themselves well to identifying a specific type of crime — such as the crime category "Killing" paired with the keyword "madness" — or to locating several examples over a certain period of time. *SH*

63. Project Wittenberg

Concordia Theological Seminary
http://www.projectwittenberg.org/

Martin Luther, a prominent sixteenth-century German theologian and reformer, wrote extensively about faith and religious doctrine. His writings helped to ignite the Protestant Reformation and found the Lutheran church. This collection of his writings, offering key Reformation texts and primary sources, is the largest online collection in English. Nearly all of Luther's well-known writings are here in their entirety: *The 95 Theses* (1517), *On the Liberty of a Christian* (1520), the *Open Letter to the German Nobility* (1520), various Bible commentaries, *Larger* and *Smaller Catechisms,* and scores of sermons, prayers, and hymns. The site, hosted by a Lutheran theological seminary, also includes information on the history of the Lutheran church in the United States, as well as a number of nineteenth- and twentieth-century commentators on Luther and Lutheran theology. There is no keyword search available, but the search function on most web browsers helps users locate words within longer texts. *MPH*

64. Salem Witch Trials Documentary Archive

University of Virginia

http://etext.virginia.edu/salem/witchcraft/

Interpretations of the Salem witch trials, one of the most widely known episodes in American history, have changed over time. Scholars have explained the accusations as the result of economic tensions, the expression of misogyny, and as the mechanism by which a community can manufacture solidarity through the politics of exclusion. These materials pertaining to the 160 women and men accused of witchcraft allow users to draw their own conclusions. The bulk of the documentation consists of a new transcription of the court trials of accused witches. There are also links to digital texts from six regional archives, seven maps (including one that places the nearly 300 people mentioned in the transcripts in their household locations in and around Salem), documents from the Salem Village Church *Record Book*, six texts on witchcraft published after the trials, and dozens of images illustrating representations of the trials through time, most of which are accessible under the "People" link. *NJ*

65. Topkapi Museum

Bilkent University

http://www.ee.bilkent.edu.tr/~history/topkapi.html

Islamic art, including what in the West would be considered "art" as well as "craft," subscribes to a certain aesthetic: it is neither exclusively religious nor produced only by Muslims. This website showcases more than 100 objects of Islamic art that once belonged to the powerful Ottoman dynasty. At the height of its power in the sixteenth century, the Ottoman Empire stretched from North Africa to Iran, and from the Balkans to the Arabian Peninsula. Main collections include: "Harem," "Palace Attire," "Imperial Treasury," "Books, Maps, and Calligraphy," "Miniatures," "Portraits of the Sultans," "Clocks," "Sacred Relics," "Porcelains," "Guns and Armory," and "Sections of the Palace." "Miniatures" is the richest section, with sixty-eight manuscript illustrations representing a variety of subjects, human and otherwise, that illustrate both secular and religious texts. They help to dispel the notion that there was no tradition of figural representation in Islamic art. *SAH*

66. Vistas: Visual Culture in Spanish America, 1520–1820

Dana Leibsohn, Smith College, and Barbara Mundy, Fordham University

http://www.smith.edu/vistas/index.html

Focusing on Spanish colonization of the Americas, this website emphasizes the use of visual imagery and architecture for understanding the complexity of colonization, from everyday life, to struggles for political control, to issues surrounding religion and spirituality. A gallery of 115 images of objects, buildings, sculptures, drawings,

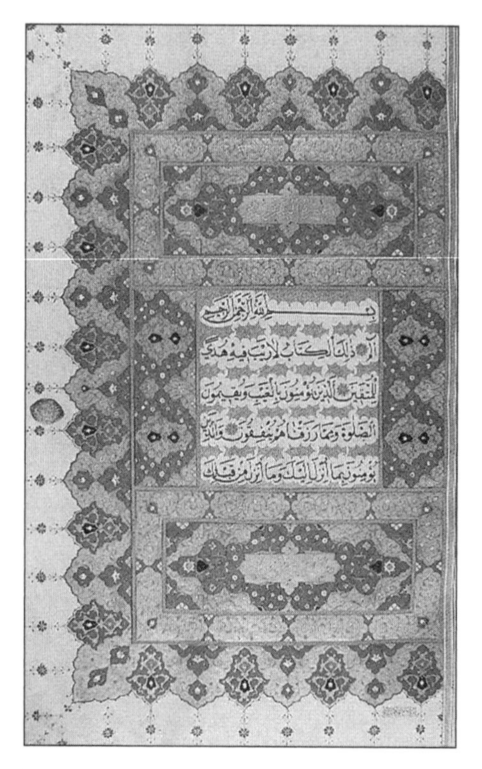

Illuminated page from the *Koran* in *Topkapi Museum* [65]. *(Photo courtesy of the Topkapi Palace Museum. Number H.S. 5, Ahmet Karahisari's Koran.)*

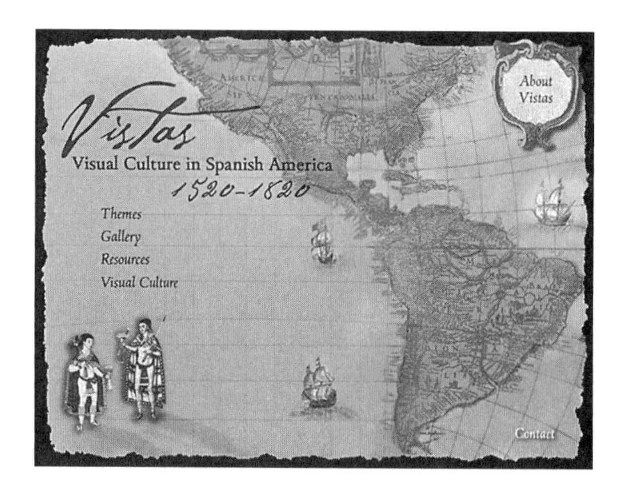

Screenshot from *Vistas: Visual Culture in Spanish America, 1520–1820* [66]. *(Courtesy of Dana Leibsohn and Barbara Mundy, Vistas: Spanish American Visual Culture, 1520-1820. http://www.smith.edu/vistas, 2005.)*

paintings, and maps from all over Spanish America — from the cosmopolitan capital of Lima, Peru, to Spanish missions in rural California — is the focal point. Each image is paired with a discussion explaining its use, origin, and significance. There are also six thematic units: "Making Sense of the Pre-Columbian," "Reckoning with Mestizaje," "Political Force of Images," "Patterns of the Everyday," "The Mechanics of an Art World," and "Otherworldly Visions." The website includes a searchable bibliography with hundreds of books written since the 1970s, resources useful for further enhancing study on visual imagery in the Americas. *JB*

More Related Websites

Africa Focus: Sights and Sounds of a Continent [127]

Afro-Louisiana History and Genealogy, 1718–1820 [69]

Avalon Project: Documents in Law, History and Diplomacy [4]

COLLAGE [73]

Collections Canada [74]

David Rumsey Collection [75]

Early Canadiana Online [76]

Excerpts from Slave Narratives [77]

From History to Herstory: Yorkshire Women's Lives Online, 1100 to the Present [79]

In Motion: The African-American Migration Experience [83]

Kyoto National Museum [13]

Mapping Margery Kempe: A Guide to Late Medieval Material and Spiritual Life [43]

Medieval and Early Modern Data Bank [45]

Medieval Illuminated Manuscripts [46]

Other Women's Voices: Translations of Women's Writing Before 1700 [47]

Tibetan and Himalayan Digital Library [147]

The Word on the Street [99]

World Art Treasures [16]

An Age of Revolutions, 1750–1914

67. Abdul-Hamid II Collection Photography Archive

Library of Congress

http://lcweb2.loc.gov/pp/ahiihtml/ahiiabt.html

In 1894, Ottoman Sultan Abdul-Hamid II presented the Library of Congress with a collection of 1,800 photographs depicting scenes within the borders of modern Turkey, as well as Ottoman holdings in Greater Syria, Greece, and modern Iraq. Most of the photos highlight the Empire's modernization, with institutions such as

Photograph of the Yeni Cami mosque in *Abdul Hamid II Photography Archive* [67]. *(Courtesy of Library of Congress Prints and Photographs Division, Washington DC, Reproduction Number: LC-USZ62-81869.)*

schools, hospitals, military barracks, medical and law schools, and fire departments featuring prominently. The Sultan included images of his residences, horses, and yachts, as well as famous landmarks such as mosques, churches, museums, and palaces from the Ottoman and Byzantine eras. The photographs, presented here in their entirety, give viewers an excellent sense of the modernizing projects the Empire focused upon during its final decades, as well as the way that Abdul-Hamid II wanted Americans to view his empire. There is a keyword search here, but the index of subjects linked to the home page must be accessed at **http://lcweb2.loc.gov/pp/ahiihtml/ahiisubjindex1.html.** *NS*

68. African American Women Writers of the 19th Century

New York Public Library

http://digital.nypl.org/schomburg/writers_aa19/

With increasing access to education and higher rates of literacy, African Americans entered a period of literary productivity in the second half of the nineteenth century. This website contains digital versions of fifty-two books and pamphlets published before 1920 by female writers from this period, many of whom were slaves or daughters of slaves. There are many genres of work represented: poetry, short stories, histories, narratives, novels, autobiographies, social criticism, and theology, as well as a few economic and philosophical treatises. The database can be browsed by title, author, or genre and is searchable by keyword, although the site provides limited background information about the authors and the era in which they wrote. The range of voices collected here will allow for an exploration of commonalities as well as differences among African American women's experiences. The texts also offer many possibilities for discovering new insights into the construction of race and racial identities. *KDL*

69. Afro-Louisiana History and Genealogy, 1718–1820

Gwendolyn Hall, Professor Emeritus, Rutgers University

http://www.ibiblio.org/laslave/

The extensive data offered through the Louisiana Slave Database and Louisiana Free Database provide information on 100,000 slaves and 4,000 freed slaves living in Louisiana and parts of present-day Mississippi, Alabama, and Florida from 1718 to 1820. Data include the names of slaves, freed slaves, slave owners, and information on slaves' origins in Africa and elsewhere. Records also provide information on plantations, skills and occupations, family relationships, involvement in conspiracies, efforts at escape, and freedom from slavery. The website presents some analysis of the data, which can be used to formulate and test hypotheses. For example, the "Mean Price by Gender" graph indicates that while the prices for enslaved men were higher than those for enslaved women after 1800, in some periods before 1800 the pattern was reversed. This can lead to questions such as what factors influenced whether buyers valued men or women more in certain periods and regions. *JB*

70. American Family Immigration History Center

The Statue of Liberty-Ellis Island Foundation, Inc.

http://www.ellisisland.org/

Records on the more than twenty-two million passengers and ship crewmembers who passed through Ellis Island between 1892 and 1924 are available through

STATES IMMIGRATION OFFICER AT PORT OF ARRIVAL

STEERAGE PASSENGERS ONLY

Arriving at Port of NEW YORK

Ship manifest record from the *American Family Immigration History Center* [70]. *(Courtesy of the American Family Immigration Center, Ellis Island, www.ellisisland.org.)*

this website. Most passengers came from Europe and Russia, although there are some records from Asia, the Caribbean, and Latin America. The website requires a free, simple registration to view detailed records that include name, residence, date of arrival, age on arrival, ethnicity, place of residence, marital status, ship of travel, place of departure, and a copy of the original ship manifest (a transcription is also available). Free membership also provides extensive contextual information about Ellis Island, immigration, and genealogical research. "Family Histories" illuminates the genealogical research experiences of six Americans of diverse ethnic backgrounds. "The Peopling of America" exhibit covers six periods from pre-1790 to 2000, with graphs, photographs, and immigration statistics geared to place of origin. Access to additional information is available for an annual fee. *KDL*

71. Around the World in the 1890s: Photographs from the World's Transportation Commission, 1894–1896

Library of Congress, American Memory

http://memory.loc.gov/ammem/wtc/wtchome.html

Between 1894 and 1896, American photographer William Henry Jackson traveled through much of eastern and southern Asia, Russia, and northern Africa for the World's Transportation Commission, an organization formed to aid American business interests abroad. This website presents more than 900 of Jackson's photographs — the bulk of the collection focusing on South Asia — which cover a wide variety of subjects not limited to forms of transportation. A central feature is the browsable list of image topics that includes popular tourist sites, locations of natural beauty, entertainment, indigenous daily life, and wildlife. Images that do highlight modes of travel, including railroads and water travel, often incorporate the local environment and people into the composition. Although these photographs are immediately useful to any discussion of nineteenth-century travel, they also provide an important comparative look at the nature of colonialism and industrialization in many of the regions to which Jackson traveled. *RD*

Photograph of Bangkok, Elephant Wat, from *Around the World in the 1890s* [71]. *(Courtesy of Library of Congress Prints and Photographs Division, World's Transportation Commission Photograph Collection, Call Number LC-W7-652.)*

72. Australian Studies Resources

University of Sydney, Scholarly Electronic Text and Image Service (SETIS)
http://setis.library.usyd.edu.au/oztexts/

This collection of Australian literary and historical texts and images, divided into ten distinct collections, features more than 200 texts comprising Australian fiction, poetry, plays, and nonfiction works, including most leading Australian literary figures of the nineteenth and twentieth centuries. More than fifty key texts record the making of the Australian Commonwealth, ranging from official records of the proceedings of federation conferences to political tracts such as feminist Catherine Helen Spence's "Woman's Place in the Commonwealth" (1900). Most of the resources range in date from the late eighteenth century to the 1920s. Especially well-represented are materials on landscape and indigenous peoples in colonial situations. The sheer variety of documents allows users to highlight resonances between political sources and associated cultural productions, such as questions of race expressed in the immediate context of debates over Australian Federation (1901). *KM*

73. COLLAGE

Guildhall Library, Guildhall Gallery of Art, and Corporation of London
http://collage.cityoflondon.gov.uk/

This collection of more than 20,000 paintings, watercolors, drawings, and sculptures provides an in-depth glimpse into the cultural history of London and London life from the fifteenth century to the present. In addition to a useful keyword search, the images can be accessed by browsing among categories that betray the immense scope of this collection, including "Abstract Ideas," "Archaeology and Architecture," "Artist," "Engraver," "History," "Leisure," "Military and War," "Natural World," "People," "Politics," "Religion and Belief," "Society," and "Trade and Industry." The images are also organized into several virtual exhibitions: "Henry Dixon's London," "London's Railways," "Children in Painting," "Victorian Paintings," "Landscapes and Seascapes," "Tudor London," "London and London Life," and "The London That Never Was." All images are cross-referenced, with links to broad categories (such as "Street Life," "Dress," and "Food and Tableware") listed at the bottom of the screen, making this collection useable even for those unfamiliar with British history. (Note that when enlarged, images bear a watermarked "C" unless purchased.) *WH*

74. Collections Canada

National Library and Archives Canada
http://www.collectionscanada.ca/website/index-e.html

Soon after the fur trade was established in New France, French Jesuit missionaries began to arrive. From 1632 through most of the seventeenth century, the missionaries produced roughly 1,800 pages of accounts. These documents, among the major works used to recreate the early history of French Canada, are included at this mega-website, along with hundreds of thousands of other sources relevant to the political, economic, social, and cultural history of Canada. Sorting the materials by topic gives a feel for their vastness — everything from "Aboriginal Peoples" to

"War and Military" to "UFOs" is included. Four thousand images from *Canadian Illustrated News,* published in Montreal between 1869 and 1883, portray local, national, and international news, depicting topics from events and people in the Middle East, Asia, and Europe to local industry and agricultural techniques. Audio files include historical recordings, sheet music, and oral histories. Videos include newsreels and interviews. Finally, the 400,000 photographs included in the "Images Canada" exhibit document an enormous spectrum of topics in Canada's history, from gypsies to coronations, and from tea parties to mine explosions. *KDL, NJ*

75. David Rumsey Collection

Cartography Associates

http://www.davidrumsey.com/

Maps, especially those containing large amounts of detailed information, are particularly suited to digitization, which allows for close-up viewing impossible in print format. This website — one of the most comprehensive historical map collections online — boasts close to 16,000 high-resolution historical maps that can be viewed with incredible clarity through the website's "Insight Browser." The maps are drawn primarily from world atlases published between the eighteenth and early twentieth centuries, but also include globes, maritime charts, manuscript maps, children's maps, and school geographies. The regional focus of the collection is on rare maps of the Americas, though maps of Africa, Asia, Oceania, and several world maps are included. Maps are fully searchable by country, state, publication, author, date, title, event, subject, and keyword. A general search on "Africa" produces close to 200 maps that could be used to chart the course of Western knowledge about the continent over the course of the nineteenth century. *KDL*

76. Early Canadiana Online

Canadiana.org

http://canadiana.org/eco.php?doc=projects

Canada's early political history is the focus of this vast collection of Canadian periodicals, official publications, parliamentary debates, records of early governors general, and documents on the Hudson Bay Company. The website also includes a substantial amount of information on women's history in nineteenth-century Canada (browse by

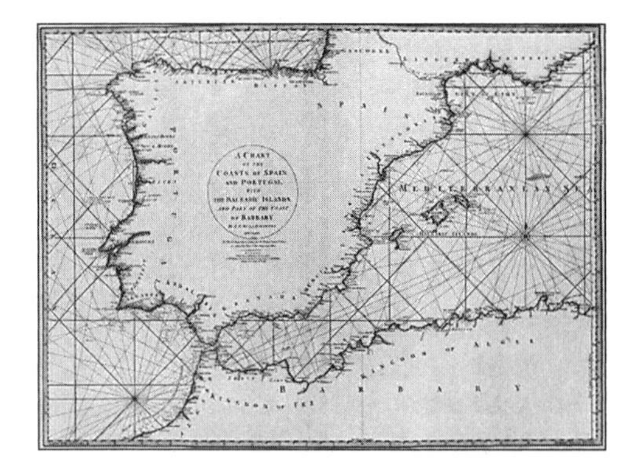

Map of Spain, Portugal, and Barbary in the *David Rumsey Collection* [75]. *(Courtesy of the David Rumsey Map Collection, www.davidrumsey.com.)*

"Collection" and then by "Women's History"), with access to nearly 700 texts, including diaries, novels, travel writings, recipe books, histories, parliamentary acts and debates, medical and religious tracts, and sermons, allowing users to reconstruct the types of experiences that (largely middle-class) women underwent during this period of Canada's national development. Materials could be used to study the construction of both feminine virtue and vice within a particular historical context. Also accessible through "Search" is information on Canadian literature, French Canada, and native studies. A subscription is required to access the browse list and several other collection features, but many resources are available at no cost. *NJ, KDL*

77. Excerpts from Slave Narratives

Steven Mintz, University of Houston

http://www.vgskole.net/prosjekt/slavrute/primary.htm

Unadorned and easy to navigate, this comprehensive website contains forty-six first-person accounts of slavery and African life dating from 1682 to 1937. Each document is introduced with an illustrative sentence or short paragraph that describes the historical context. There are both recognizable and unknown actors in this website: former slaves such as Olaudah Equiano, Frederick Douglass, and Harriet Tubman, as well as white abolitionists such as John Brown express forceful, if familiar, condemnations of slavery. In addition, there are unheralded historical voices that not only speak poignantly, but also reflect different perspectives. For example, a ship doctor presents a searing report on the Middle Passage; a slave husband writes an anguished letter to his wife after she was sold; and a black social reformer protests the cruel punishments of slave owners. When taken together, the assembled testimonies present slavery as a deeply entrenched institution that provoked a wide range of compelling commentary. *BC, RE*

78. Formosa

Reed College

http://academic.reed.edu/formosa/

European and American travelers to Taiwan in the nineteenth century created woodcuts, maps, images, and travelogues about the people who inhabited the land they called "Formosa." This collection offers several hundred maps, images (primarily of architecture, landscape, art objects, people, and boats), and travelogues, as well as a small sample of linguistic data. Together, these materials serve as a window into the Orientalist mindset that shaped the experiences of European and American travelers, creating an image of Asia in contrast to the West's own image of itself.

Screenshot from *Formosa* [78]. *(Courtesy of Douglas Fix and the Computing and Information Services, Reed College.)*

Most of the firsthand accounts pay particular attention to the aboriginal peoples of Taiwan — as opposed to the Chinese residents whose social and cultural patterns had come to predominate in most areas. The visual and textual representations of Taiwanese aborigines closely resemble representations of other "primitive" populations that nineteenth-century Europeans and Americans encountered in their travels around the globe. *BP*

79. From History to Herstory: Yorkshire Women's Lives Online, 1100 to the Present

West Yorkshire Archive Service, United Kingdom

http://www.historytoherstory.org.uk/

Although women have often been omitted from the historical record, they were active at all levels of society. This website illustrates that point, aiming to raise the profile of women in both popular and scholarly understandings of history. It showcases the lives of women in Yorkshire, England, from the second century C.E. to the present day, through 85,000 images and documents. Among the women featured are well-known figures, such as Charlotte, Emily, and Anne Bronte (Victorian novelists) and Anne Lister (a prominent early-nineteenth-century woman whose coded diaries document her life, travels, and lesbian love affairs), though the website also includes material on many relatively obscure women. The resources are organized alphabetically and are fully searchable, allowing users to uncover the lives of individuals and groups, or to trace themes, such as the role of wealth and status in determining how women might transgress contemporary norms and values throughout the centuries. *KM*

80. Gertrude Bell Project

Tyne Library, University of Newcastle

http://www.gerty.ncl.ac.uk/

Gertrude Bell, born in England in 1868 and educated at Oxford, spent much of her life traveling and recording her travels through photographs, diaries, and letters. Before 1903, she made two around-the-world voyages and hiked the Alps. Afterwards, Bell became increasingly involved in the archaeological and political affairs of the Middle East; as the only woman invited by Winston Churchill to the Cairo Conference of 1921, she was instrumental in drawing the boundary lines of Iraq. This collection offers 600 letters that Bell wrote to her parents, sixteen diaries

Gertrude Bell
1868-1926
The Robinson Library
UNIVERSITY OF NEWCASTLE

Gertrude Bell

Gertrude Bell (1868-1926) was born in Washington, in what was then Co. Durham, but, when she was very young, she moved with her family to Redcar. She was educated first of all at home, and then at school in London; finally, in a time when it was not at all usual for a woman to have a university education, she went to Oxford to read history, and, at the age of twenty and after only two years study, she left with a first-class degree. In the years immediately following, she spent time on the social round in London and Yorkshire,

Screenshot from *Gertrude Bell Project* [80]. *(Permission of the University Librarian, Robinson Library, Newcastle University, Newcastle upon Tyne.)*

(covering her travels from 1877 to 1919), 7,000 photographs taken between 1900 and 1918 (which include many archaeological sites that were subsequently destroyed), and about forty packets of miscellaneous documents. Together, these materials illuminate the larger themes of women travelers and their writing, as well as the timely topic of Western intervention in the Middle East, in particular Iraq. *KM*

81. Harappa: The Indus Valley and the Raj in India and Pakistan

Omar Khan, Jim McCall, and Andrew Deonarine

http://www.harappa.com

This website presents one of the most impressive online collections of South Asian primary sources. Materials concentrate on two distinct periods in the history of South Asia: the Indus Valley Civilization (ca. 2000–1500 B.C.E.) and the much more recent transition from the Raj to Independence and Partition. The 270 images in three "Indus Tour" slide shows provide a comprehensive introduction to this ancient culture and include maps and reconstructive drawings. More than 700 nineteenth-century photographs, prints, engravings, postcards, and lithographs depict colonialism, British views of India, and the British desire to attract more countrymen (or, more specifically, countrywomen) to the subcontinent during the Raj. Of particular note is the selection of newsreel footage depicting important leaders, such as Gandhi, Nehru, and Jinnah, as well as key moments in the early history of modern South Asia. These materials also provide valuable insight into American and European representations of the Indian subcontinent. *RD*

82. Historical Maps, Perry-Castañada Library Map Collection

University of Texas at Austin

http://www.lib.utexas.edu/maps/historical/index.html

Close to 1,000 historical maps are offered through this website, most of which date from the nineteenth and early twentieth centuries and are drawn from historical atlases and magazines published within the U.S. or by the U.S. State Department or Central Intelligence Agency. Thus, these maps are especially effective as tools for understanding how the U.S. has viewed the world. The collection is divided by geographic region. "Historical Maps of the United States" — the largest section represented — includes several hundred military maps (including thirty Pacific Theater maps from World War II), as well as several maps documenting Native American locations and languages and many more showing Westward Expansion. "Americas" includes maps from Canada to Argentina. All maps are accompanied by detailed bibliographic information (source, author, year of publication), and thus might also be useful for projects on the history of mapmaking and historical atlases. *KDL*

83. In Motion: The African-American Migration Experience

Schomburg Center for Research in Black Culture

http://www.inmotionaame.org/home.cfm

Migration, both forced and voluntary, remains a prominent theme in African American history. This website is built around the history of thirteen African

American migration experiences, including many in the fifteenth through nineteenth centuries: "The Transatlantic Slave Trade" (1450s–1867), "Runaway Journeys" (1630s–1865), "The Domestic Slave Trade" (1760s–1865), "Colonization and Emigration" (1783–1910s), "Haitian Immigration" (1791–1809), "The Western Migration" (1840s–1970), and "The Northern Migration" (1840s–1890). Twentieth-century migrations include "The Great Migration" (1916–1930), "The Second Great Migration" (1940–1970), "Caribbean Immigration" (1900–present), "Return South Migration" (1970–present), "Haitian Immigration in the Twentieth Century" (1970–present), and "African Immigration" (1970–present). More than 16,500 pages of texts and 8,300 illustrations are included, as well as maps. One strength of these sources is that they draw equal attention to commonly discussed migration experiences, such as the domestic slave trade and the Great Migration, and to those that are less studied, such as twentieth-century Caribbean immigration. *KDL*

84. Japanese Old Photographs in Bakumatsu-Meiji Period

Nagasaki University Library

http://hikoma.lb.nagasaki-u.ac.jp/en/

The second half of the nineteenth century was tumultuous and significant in Japan's history, marking Japan's confrontation with Western imperialism, the overthrow of the feudal Tokugawa regime in 1868, and the rapid formation of a modern nation-state. This period coincided with developments in photographic technology, and, as a result, when Western diplomats, missionaries, and merchants came to Japan, they often brought cameras. The Japanese began taking pictures as well. This collection represents a large sample of the photographs taken during this era. Many landscape photographs are included, but there are also hundreds of images of Japanese people, such as farmers planting rice, a blind beggar on a city street, and three awkwardly posed samurai in full armor, as well as many staged pictures of Japanese women, particularly geisha (a favorite subject of Western photographers). These photo-

Photograph of a woman painting a *yamato-e* from *Japanese Old Photographs in Bakumatsu-Meiji Period* [84]. *(Photo courtesy of the Nagasaki University Library.)*

graphs can add a visual dimension to a discussion of Western perspectives on Asian people and culture: the Japan they depict is one that stands in clear contrast to the self-image of nineteenth-century Europe. *BP*

85. Journeys in Time, 1809–1822: The Diaries of Lachlan and Elizabeth Macquarie

Macquarie University, Sydney, and State Library of New South Wales, Australia

http://www.lib.mq.edu.au/all/journeys/menu.html

Over the thirteen years that Lachlan Macquarie was governor of colonial New South Wales in the early 1800s, he and his wife, Elizabeth, kept detailed diaries describing their public and private lives. This website presents full transcripts of the diaries as they chart a significant moment in the history of European expansion. Macquarie's governorship ushered in the consolidation of European colonies in Australia. He embarked on an ambitious program of public works, redesigned Sydney, and fostered social reformation and the emergence of free institutions in the convict colony. His diary entries shed light not only on the nature of British imperial expansion in the Pacific and the business of colonial governance, but also on the larger themes of travel writing and colonial encounters. Most importantly, the inclusion of the perspectives of both Lachlan and Elizabeth Macquarie allows users to examine the differences between public and private and masculine and feminine perspectives in the early-nineteenth-century colonial realm. *KM*

86. Liberian Letters

University of Virginia, Electronic Text Center

http://etext.lib.virginia.edu/subjects/liberia/

Founded in 1816, the American Colonization Society advocated sending manumitted slaves and free blacks living in the United States to Africa. The first "repatriated" black emigrants landed in Liberia in 1821. They were not prepared to till the land and the displaced local Africans were hostile. Most importantly, the American-born blacks were highly susceptible to malaria and yellow fever. This website offers the opinions of surviving pioneers, including six compelling letters authored in 1834 and 1835 by Samson Ceasar, a freed slave, who wrote to David Haselden and Henry Westfall of Buchannon, Virginia. An additional forty-four letters were sent by former slaves of James Hunter Terrell to Terrell's executor, Dr. James Minor, between 1857 and 1866. The diverse letters not only reflect the complex bonds between former slaves and masters, but also underscore the persistently unequal relationship. *BC, RE*

87. Liberty, Equality, Fraternity

CHNM, George Mason University, and ASHP, City University of New York

http://chnm.gmu.edu/revolution

This brief but comprehensive overview of the French Revolution from its social causes through the Napoleonic experience is based on a collection of more than 600 images, texts, maps, and songs. Clicking on "Browse" allows users to view the collection by category: "Images," "Texts," "Maps," "Songs." In addition to a "Timeline" and "Glossary," the "Search" feature is especially useful. For example, a search on the economic conditions of the peasantry produces nine potential resources that describe conditions on the eve of the Revolution. With some additional context, these sources could produce a wonderfully focused examination of the conditions of the French peasantry during the last years of the *ancien régime*. Indeed, the collection is well-contextualized in the "Explore" section that highlights important aspects of the period through in-depth scholarly essays, several of which shed light on topics that are sometimes underrepresented in textbooks, such as "Women and the Revolution" and "Slavery and the Haitian Revolution." *WH*

88. Mexican-American War and the Media

Professor Linda Arnold, Virginia Tech University
http://www.history.vt.edu/MxAmWar/index.htm

This growing archive provides more than 5,000 newspaper articles related to the Mexican-American War as well as paintings, prints, and illustrations. The transcribed articles represent five newspapers from the United States and England,

Photograph of indigenous men from *Mexico: From Empire to Revolution* [89]. *(Research Library, The Getty Research Institute, Los Angeles, California (99.R.17).)*

spanning the period from 1845 — when the United States annexed Texas — through 1848, when Mexico surrendered and the Treaty of Guadalupe Hidalgo was signed. The contrast between coverage of the war in the United States and England is particularly striking. *The Times* of London fulminated against the immorality of slavery and of the Southern scheme to annex Texas as a slave state, while exposing America's imperialist ambitions as, among other things, an attempt to shore up the nation's fragile stability through the escape valve of Western migration. By contrast, newspapers from Maryland and West Virginia did not examine the issue of slavery, at least in the articles included here. The website provides a comprehensive bibliography on the war, but does not offer any historical background or contextualization beyond links to related materials. *MK*

89. Mexico: From Empire to Revolution

Getty Research Institute

http://www.getty.edu/research/conducting_research/digitized_collections/mexico/html/index.html

The decades between 1857 and 1923 were crucial in Mexican history. This photographic archive presents the work of more than thirty photographers, both Mexican and non-Mexican, active during this period. Topics include the French Intervention in Mexico during the 1860s, the victory of Benito Juarez and the execution of Emperor Maximilian, and daily life during the Porfirian dictatorship (1876–1911). The "History" section presents the photographs in chronological order as well as a basic narrative history. While the narrative provides a useful context for the photographs, the version of Mexican history it presents is quite simplistic. For example, while the historical narrative depicts the Mexican Revolution as a simple class conflict, the photographs suggest a more complex reality. Though the leaders of revolutionary factions were drawn from different social classes, the masses who followed these leaders into battle were not so easily distinguished by class, but rather by ethnicity, culture, and geographical region. *MK*

90. Mysteries in Canadian History

University of Victoria

http://www.canadianmysteries.ca/indexen.html

Nine mysteries come to life through this website that re-investigates unsolved (or mis-solved) historical crimes. Each case begins with an introduction, and then invites users to create their own narratives based on more than 200 primary sources for each story, including images, court documents, newspaper articles, diary entries, maps, books, letters, and government documents. Users may begin by focusing on "solving" the crime itself, but along the way will be drawn into the consideration of historical practices (critical reading, evaluating evidence, understanding different perspectives, drawing conclusions), as well as important themes in Canadian history, such as indigenous-white relations, western settlement, and immigration. Viewers are introduced to this history through the stories of particular historical persona often marginalized from the traditional grand narrative — a black slave executed for starting a fire in Montreal in 1734; a family of Irish Catholics who were massacred in London, Ontario, in the 1880s; and a group of dissident Russians who settled in western Canada in the early twentieth century. *NJ*

Drawing of a Canadian couple from *Mysteries in Canadian History* [90]. *(City of Montreal Archives.)*

91. Pauline Johnson Archive

McMaster University

http://www.humanities.mcmaster.ca/~pjohnson/home.html

Emily Pauline Johnson, the daughter of a Mohawk father and an English mother, was one of Canada's most successful entertainers at the turn of the twentieth century. She wanted to reshape white society's perceptions of contemporary indigenous culture, even though her own experience of this culture was highly atypical. As a young woman, Johnson began writing poetry, short stories, and essays that treated the experiences and history of Canadian natives in the Great Lakes region and the Canadian west. Resources include transcriptions of Johnson's writings, scanned manuscript documents, contemporary reviews of her work, letters from fans and critics, short video clips of Johnson's dress and a reading of one of her poems, and more than seventy photographs, postcards, and reproductions of brochures and programs. This website provides a variety of sources and perspectives through which to examine the life of this remarkable turn-of-the-century native Canadian writer, as well as the history of women writers, indigenous people, and racial identity in this often neglected Canadian context. *NJ*

92. Slaves and the Courts, 1740–1860

Library of Congress, American Memory

http://memory.loc.gov/ammem/sthtml/sthome.html

This collection of 105 documents published between 1772 and 1889 deals with the legal experiences of slaves and the legal aspects of slavery in the United States and Great Britain. Documents include arguments, examinations, reports, testimonies, and other materials related to cases involving slaves, slave traders, and abolitionists.

Photograph from the *Pauline Johnson Archive* [91]. *(William Ready Division of Archives and Research Collections, McMaster University Library.)*

Famous cases such as *Somerset v. Stewart*, the *Amistad* case, the *Dred Scott Decision*, and the trials of the rebel Denmark Vesey, the abolitionist William Lloyd Garrison, and the abolitionist and rebel John Brown are included, as are lesser-known cases. A special exhibit highlights the slave code of the District of Columbia. Little contextual information is provided, so users might consult *From Slavery to Freedom: A History of African Americans* by John Hope Franklin and Alfred A. Moss, Jr. (2000), or *Hard Road to Freedom: The Story of African America* by James Oliver Horton and Lois E. Horton (2001). *JB*

93. South Seas Voyaging and Cross-Cultural Encounters in the Pacific

The National Library of Australia, and the Centre for Cross-Cultural Research at the Australian National University, Canberra

http://southseas.nla.gov.au/

Between 1760 and 1800, Captain James Cook made three trips to the Pacific Ocean, mapping the eastern coast of Australia and circumnavigating New Zealand. This resource on the history of European voyaging and cross-cultural encounters in the Pacific focuses on Cook's first voyage (1768 to 1771). Four key narratives associated with this voyage are provided: the journals kept by Cook, by botanist Joseph Banks, and by artist Sydney Parkinson, and a published work by John Hawkesworth. Three supplementary texts address European reactions to and indigenous views of the voyages. More than twenty maps, an encyclopedia, a dictionary, and a bibliography serve to contextualize the travel accounts. Journal entries are annotated with cross-references to the encyclopedia. One entry from Cook's journal (14 April 1769) includes cross-references to concepts such as "theft, in Maohi society," allowing for fruitful discussions of the class dimensions of theft in European and Maohi society. *KM*

94. South Texas Border, 1900–1920: Photographs from the Robert Runyon Collection

University of Texas and American Memory, Library of Congress

http://memory.loc.gov/ammem/award97/txuhtml/runyhome.html

Commercial photographer Robert Runyon photographed the south Texas borderlands extensively during the 1910s and 1920s. His images represent a valuable visual record of life in that region and provide an important window onto a relatively understudied phase of the Mexican Revolution. This website provides minimal historical context for the 8,000 images it contains. Individual images are accompanied only by the most basic descriptions, such as "barricades," "soldiers," or "Generals Pablo Gonzalez and Jesus Carranza visiting hospital," and are often undated. Nevertheless, the images are clear and sharp, and ripe for analysis. For example, the impressive clarity of the photograph, "Maria Gonzalez and soldaderas," makes it possible to analyze the flag, clothing, weaponry, and facial expressions of three female soldiers who served the Constitutionalist army during the Mexican Revolution. Other fruitful topics include the composition of the Constitutionalist army and the nature of revolutionary justice on the border. *MK*

Photograph of Maria Gonzalez with soldaderas from *South Texas Border* [94]. *(Permission from Center for American History, University of Texas at Austin.)*

95. Spanish-American War in Motion Pictures

American Memory, Library of Congress

http://memory.loc.gov/ammem/sawhtml/sawhome.html

The Spanish-American War was one of the first wars captured on film. This website features sixty-eight motion pictures of the war and the Philippine Revolution produced by the Edison Manufacturing Company and the American Mutoscope and Biograph Company between 1898 and 1901. The films include footage of troops, ships, notable figures, parades, and battle reenactments shot in the United States, Cuba, and the Philippines. Theodore Roosevelt's Rough Riders are featured alongside footage of the *USS Maine* in Havana harbor. "Special Presentation" puts the motion pictures in chronological order and brief essays provide historical context. "Collection Connections" provides thought-provoking activities and essay topics. This glimpse at early film footage enhances our understanding of the fledgling technology, and offers a way to better understand U.S. imperialism at the turn of the century. The films expose some of the ways in which the birth of cinema emerged alongside, and shaped, changing ideas of gender, race, sexuality, and nation. *MK*

96. Views of the Famine

Steve Taylor

http://adminstaff.vassar.edu/sttaylor/FAMINE/

From approximately 1845 to 1851, Ireland witnessed a potato famine that claimed close to one million lives, spurred waves of mass emigration, and permanently changed the social, cultural, and economic structure of Irish society. This website presents hundreds of images, cartoons, and articles about the famine from several Irish and British publications. Articles are drawn from the *Illustrated London News*, the *Cork Examiner* (Ireland), and the *Pictorial Times* (London). Cartoons come from *Punch*, a London magazine. Also included is an 1847 travel narrative: *Narrative of a Journey From Oxford To Skibberdean During the Year of the Irish Famine.* A particularly interesting issue that these materials raise is whether or not Britain's delayed response in providing material aid furthered Irish suffering. There is little historical contextualization provided, but the breadth of materials allows users to explore first-hand the causes of and responses to the famine and the ways in which it changed Ireland. *KDL*

97. Women's Library: Suffrage Banners Collection

Arts and Humanities Data Service (AHDS)

http://vads.ahds.ac.uk/collections/FSB.html

The women's suffrage movement in Britain saw a shift in strategy in the early twentieth century. While still focused on influencing parliament, the movement began to pay greater attention to methods designed to alert and shape public opinion. Banners and associated artwork produced by artist-based suffrage organizations were particularly suited to this goal. This collection offers hundreds of these banners, useful for examining the choice of heroic figures in the iconography, the ways in which professional women were represented, or the use of political theater through

Banner from *Women's Library* [97]. *(Women's Library Suffrage Banners Collection, 1908–1914. Courtesy of London Metropolitan University.)*

photographs of the banners being employed in demonstrations. A key disadvantage to the website is that there is no browse function, thus requiring users to know what search terms will be productive. Non-specialists using this website may find Lisa Tickner, *The Spectacle of Women: Imagery of the Suffrage Campaign 1907–14*, helpful for providing necessary background information and key topics. *KM*

98. Women's Travel Writing, 1830–1930: Women's Studies Digitization Project

University of Minnesota, Wilson Library Electronic Text Research Center

http://etrc.lib.umn.edu/womtrav.htm

This collection of travel writings by more than twenty-five women who wrote between 1830 and 1930 provides fascinating impressions of daily life, religious customs, and political realities of various locales around Africa, Latin America, East Asia, Canada, and Europe. All authors came from middle- or upper-class backgrounds and traveled in a variety of capacities, including as botanists, ethnologists, artists, political activists, and wives of diplomats. These texts can be interpreted in the framework of the neo-colonial era of the late nineteenth and early twentieth centuries and the growing economic and military influence of Europe and the United States in Africa, Asia, and Latin America. For example, Frances Workman, a suffragist who traveled to Algeria, perceptively records the subordination of Arabic culture in the context of French imperialism. One of the website's most useful features is that the database of texts can be searched by word, synonym, or analytic categories such as ethnicity, gender, and occupation. *NJ*

99. The Word on the Street

National Library of Scotland

http://www.nls.uk/broadsides/

The broadside, a precursor to newspapers in the seventeenth through twentieth centuries, was a one-page, mass publication often posted in public places. Initially featuring official government announcements, the broadside changed over time into a popular print medium written in various genres, including ballads, elegies, speeches, political tracts, and morality tales. This collection of 1,800 broadsides from Scotland, published between 1650 and 1910, provides a window onto political, social, and cultural history. Topics include crime, emigration, sport, and humor. Like all primary sources, broadsides represent the past in selective ways, and the time and place in which the texts were written ultimately shaped their messages. A comparison of two broadsides dealing with the execution of criminals (*The*

Last Words of James Mackpherson Murderer from 1700 and *A list of all the Horrid Murders committed by Burke . . .* from 1829) illustrates that point well, showing how the relationship of criminals to their respective communities can change over time. SH

More Related Websites

Africa Focus: Sights and Sounds of a Continent [127]

American Journeys [51]

Atlantic Slave Trade and Slave Life in the Americas: A Visual Record [52]

Australian War Memorial [102]

Avalon Project: Documents in Law, History and Diplomacy [4]

Bodleian Library Broadside Ballads [53]

British History Online [54]

Canadian Letters and Images Project [105]

Christian Classics Ethereal Library [55]

Complete Works of William Shakespeare [56]

Digital South Asia Library [6]

Gifts of Speech: Women's Speeches from Around the World [140]

Hanover Historical Texts Project [59]

Hispano Music and Culture from the Northern Rio Grande: The Juan B. Rael Collection [111]

Historic Cities: Maps and Documents [60]

Mahatma Gandhi Research and Media Service [114]

Marxists Internet Archive [115]

Medieval and Early Modern Data Bank [45]

National Museum of African Art [117]

Native American Constitution and Law Digitization Project [118]

PictureAustralia [119]

Political Database of the Americas [144]

Proceedings of the Old Bailey [62]

Project Wittenberg [63]

Tibetan and Himalayan Digital Library [147]

Timeframes [123]

Topkapi Museum [65]

Uysal-Walker Archive of Turkish Oral Narrative [149]

Virtual Shanghai: Shanghai Urban Space in Time [125]

Vistas: Visual Culture in Spanish America, 1520–1820 [66]

Visual Arts Data Services [150]

A Half-Century of Crisis and Achievement, 1900–1945

100. "A Summons To Comradeship": World War I and II Posters

University of Minnesota Libraries

http://digital.lib.umn.edu/warposters/warpost.html

Poster art shaped and reflected the nature of "total war" in the first half of the twentieth century, and remains a rich primary source for examining the political, military, social, and cultural history of World War I and World War II. This website provides

Poster from "*A Summons to Comradeship*" [100]. *(World War Poster Collection Manuscripts Division, University of Minnesota Libraries, Minneapolis, MN.)*

a database of close to 6,000 posters; those from the United States constitute the bulk of the collection, followed by posters from Great Britain, France, Czechoslovakia, the Soviet Union, Italy, and Germany. Descriptions are keyword searchable, and there are also categories for browsing. Fifteen posters under "Civilian Participation" represent one of the key components of "total war": full participation of citizens both at the front and at home. Posters can be used to examine the ways in which citizens on the home front were drawn into the war effort, as well as messages about gender and class. Other subjects include organizations, war-related social groups, and individual political leaders. *SH*

101. American Museum Congo Expedition, 1909–1915

American Museum of Natural History, Digital Library Project
http://diglib1.amnh.org

Whether deserved or not, the "Congo" evokes wonder tinged with fear. Deep in central Africa's interior, researchers spent years cataloging its mysterious natural treasures. This website presents the notes, photographs, maps, and drawings of one such expedition from 1909 to 1915, sponsored by the American Museum of Natural History and led by mammologist Herbert Lang and his assistant James Chapin. The collection contains 2,000 scanned images of specimens and art collected by Lang and Chapin; more than a dozen publications that place their discoveries, ethnographies, and diaries in historical context; and a selection of seven early sound recordings. Materials describe how Africans lived within the bounds of their ecosystem and allude to the costs of environmental degradation and social engineering wrought by Belgian King Leopold II's exploitation of rubber as a resource in the Congo. They are especially useful for considering whether Western scientific expeditions yielded more "objective" data about the colonial experience than the recorded testimony of whites in colonial governments. *BC*

102. Australian War Memorial

Australian War Memorial, Canberra
http://www.awm.gov.au/index.asp

From the Anglo-Maori Wars in New Zealand (1860–1866) to the most recent war in Iraq, Australia has participated in many regional and international conflicts. This website provides information about the history of Australia at war, through primary and secondary material located in the "Collection Databases" and "Biographical Databases." These databases contain more than 4,000 works of art, 200,000 photographs, 3,500 films, 350 sound recordings, 8,200 private records, 400 oral history transcripts, and 2,000 heraldry and technology items. Thematic approaches to understanding these sources in the context of world history, such as memorializing war, war diaries, or the role of women in war, are possible through advanced searching. Particular campaigns presented from the Australian perspective might be compared with their place in other national narratives. The collection also presents primary sources for each of Australia's leaders, which lends itself to analyzing the connections between war and ideas of leadership and nation. *KM*

103. British Cartoon Archive

British Cartoon Archive at the University of Kent

http://opal.ukc.ac.uk/cartoonx-cgi/ccc.py

This collection of more than 120,000 cartoons published in British newspapers over the past 200 years claims to be the largest cartoon database in the world. The cartoons shed light on almost any topic imaginable in British political, economic, social, and cultural history. Searches on "Africa," "India," and "empire" produce thousands of cartoons revealing views of British foreign relations, colonialism, and decolonization. A search for "disease" reveals the deep trauma that the worldwide influenza epidemic of 1917 caused in British society. More than 5,000 cartoons address Britain's involvement in twentieth-century world wars. The "Artist Index" provides brief bibliographies of all 521 cartoonists represented in the database, and allows users to trace the development of single cartoonists over time. Though there is little additional historical context, several records provide transcriptions of newspaper articles accompanying the cartoons. In addition, each cartoon enlarges to full screen, allowing for detailed examination of these rich historical sources. *KDL*

104. British Voices from South Asia

T. Harry Williams Oral History Center, Louisiana State University

http://www.lib.lsu.edu/special/exhibits/india/intro.htm

Between 1857, when Britain established formal rule of the Indian subcontinent, and 1947, when that rule ended, thousands of British citizens participated in the colonial experience in India. This website captures their voices through forty interviews conducted with civil servants, military men, and their families. These unique viewpoints explore a variety of themes, including motivations that led these individuals to seek out life in the colonies. The website also provides details about military expeditions, leisure activities, and domestic routines; the divide that separated the British from the South Asians and the regrets and rationalizations that often accompanied this socially enforced division; and views on the emergence of India, Bangladesh, and Pakistan as independent states. These transcribed interviews are accompanied by 100 images, ranging from paintings of Indians to photographs of daily British life and household objects, that serve to contextualize the individual stories and place them within the broader setting of British colonialism in India. *RD*

105. Canadian Letters and Images Project

Malaspina University, History Department

http://www.canadianletters.ca/

The personal side of warfare is often ignored in discussions of military conflict, but this archive, in contrast, presents thousands of documents surrounding individual Canadian soldiers' experiences. The collection is divided chronologically: "Pre-1914," "World War I," "World War II," "Korea," and "Post-Korea," although most materials are from the World War I and World War II eras. Materials are also presented by individual soldier. Documents include more than 6,000 letters as well as thousands of postcards, photographs, excerpts from personal journals, newspaper clippings, and poems. Official documents include personal records, such as marriage licenses and birth certificates, and official army documents. Most documents are collected directly from soldiers and their families, and are often unavailable elsewhere. The "Advanced Search" function is still in development, but a keyword search is available and the contents of each collection are well summarized, making it relatively easy to find specific documents. KDL

106. Democracy at War: Canadian Newspapers and the Second World War

The Canadian War Museum

http://www.warmuseum.ca/cwm/newspapers/intro_e.html

World War II was covered extensively in Canadian newspapers, including *The Hamilton Spectator* (Ontario), *The Globe and Mail* (Toronto), *The Toronto Telegram*, and *The Toronto Daily Star*. This website presents a searchable database of 144,000 newspaper articles (including some from the *New York Times* and *The Times* of London), providing a comprehensive introduction to the political, economic, and social causes and consequences of World War II through contemporary documents. In order to facilitate browsing, the website is partitioned into several sections: "Canada and the War," "Operations," and "The Holocaust." Each section contains articles grouped under diverse topics that allow users to explore Canada's view of and participation in the war, as well as a more general perspective on the major campaigns and issues surrounding the war. "Operations," for example, presents articles on the Burma campaigns, the North African campaign, and the invasion of China. Each topic is preceded by several paragraphs of historical contextualization. KDL

107. East Asian Collection

University of Wisconsin Digital Collections

http://digicoll.library.wisc.edu/EastAsian/

This portal provides access to three archives of black-and-white photographs: "The China in the 1930s Collection/Tianjin Collection," "The Holmes Welch Collection," and "The William Hervie Dobson Collection." Welch was a well-known scholar of modern Chinese religion whose photographs capture various aspects of Chinese Buddhist monastic life and practice as well as the details and varieties of Chinese Buddhist architecture. Dobson was an American Presbyterian missionary and doctor who turned his lens upon the urban and rural milieus in which he simultaneously practiced medicine and evangelized. Together, these three collections contain nearly 500 images of Chinese soldiers and military practices, the Sino-Japanese Conflict (1937–1945), Buddhism, and rural and urban daily life, from beggars to officials. A full bibliographic record accompanies each photograph. These images can be used to study the social, religious, cultural, and geographic diversity of China in the first half of the twentieth century, as well as the impact of momentous events upon different regions and social groups. MC

108. Frontera Collection of Mexican American Music

UCLA, Arhoolie Foundation, Los Tigres Del Norte Foundation

http://digital.library.ucla.edu/frontera/

This collection of commercially produced Mexican American vernacular music is the largest of its kind. The project is currently digitizing 30,000 phonograph recordings from the larger collection of 100,000 items. The music, originally published throughout the twentieth century, is primarily in Spanish and varies widely in style and genre, including lyric songs, *canciones*, *boleros*, *rancheras*, *sones*, instrumental music, and the first recordings of *norteño* music. Also included are several politically motivated speeches and comedy skits. A browsable list of subjects shows that "love" (*e.g.*, unrequited love, adultery, regrets), "war" (*e.g.*, Mexican Revolution, World Wars I and II, Korean War,), and "praise" (of country, guitar, mother) are common themes in the collection. Unfortunately, the songs are available only in fifty-second sound clips to users outside of the UCLA campus; however, users interested in gaining full access to a select group of songs for research are encouraged to contact the website's administrators. *KDL*

109. G. I. Jones, Photographic Archive of Southeastern Nigerian Art and Culture

John C. McCall, Southern Illinois University

http://mccoy.lib.siu.edu/jmccall/jones/

G. I. Jones, a South African-born anthropologist, photographed the people of the Igbo-speaking regions of southeastern Nigeria during his twenty-year tenure as an administrative officer in the British colonial service. These 350 photographs, taken in the 1930s, are a small sample drawn from his extensive archive. Depicted here are carvings, pots, drums, and masks, including masks worn as people participated in dances, festivals, and initiation rites. Many of the images show masked performers amidst their audience, graphically representing the interaction between art form and viewer. The images are remarkable for their size, brightness, and clarity, and the photography is exemplary from a technical standpoint. The broad range of material culture represented makes this a powerful resource for examining many topics in African history, including indigenous religions and colonialism, or as a companion to the novel *Things Fall Apart* by Nigerian writer Chinua Achebe. *EAP*

Photograph of a Nigerian dancer at an Ogbukele festival from *G. I. Jones, Photographic Archive of Southeastern Nigerian Art and Culture* [109]. *(Reproduced by permission of University of Cambridge Museum of Archaeology & Anthropology (P.61392.GIJ).)*

Gate seen from the balcony of a building at Nanhai Gong Yuan from *Hedda Morrison Photographs of China* [110]. *(Hedda Morrison Collection, Harvard-Yenching Library; copyright President and Fellows of Harvard College.)*

110. Hedda Morrison Photographs of China, 1933–1946

Raymond Lum, Harvard-Yenching Library, Harvard University, USA

http://hcl.harvard.edu/libraries/harvard-yenching/collections/morrison/

German-born photographer Hedda Hammer Morrison (1908–1991) lived in Beijing (then known as Peking) from 1933 to 1946. This collection of 5,000 black-and-white photographs taken by Morrison documents daily life, trade, handicrafts, landscapes, commercial and religious practices, and architectural structures that may have changed or been destroyed over the course of the twentieth century. All of the photographs depict subjects in and around Beijing and China's northern provinces, and include many images of imperial gardens, Buddhist temples, street scenes, and Buddhist nuns in Beijing. Additional photographs focus on the Temple of Heaven (an imperial state altar) and the Forbidden City. These photographs provide an important window into Chinese material culture and social customs during the Republican era (1911–1949). To locate images in this collection, click on the "Search VIA" link and enter the term "Hedda Morrison" in the "Name" field. *MC*

111. Hispano Music and Culture from the Northern Rio Grande: The Juan B. Rael Collection

Library of Congress, American Memory Project

http://memory.loc.gov/ammem/rghtml/rghome.html

In the early 1940s, Juan B. Rael, a linguist and folklorist at Stanford University, traveled to rural northern New Mexico and southern Colorado to document the religious and secular music of the region's Spanish-speaking residents. This website presents 146 of Rael's sound recordings, of *alabados* (hymns), folk drama, wedding songs, and dance tunes, by fifteen performers, for a total of eight hours of recordings. Descriptive information about the title, performers, genre, instrumentation, location and date of recording, and other brief notes about the music accompany each tune. The website also presents Rael's recording logs, three publications relating to the collection, a map of the region, and four background essays on Rael and northern New Mexican culture that provide important contextual information. All songs can be searched or browsed by title and performer. Most are available in MP3, RealAudio, and WAV formats. *KDL*

Photograph of Philip Ahn from the *Korean American Digital Archive* [112]. *(Reproduced by permission of USC Korean American Digital Archive.)*

112. Korean American Digital Archive

University of Southern California

http://www.usc.edu/libraries/collections/korean_american/

Thousands of primary materials presented at this website, including documents compiled by Korean American organizations, personal papers, more than 1,900 photographs, and around 180 interviews, address the experiences of Koreans in the United States between 1903 and 1965. The materials run the gamut from organizational memos and other official documents to personal letters, wedding programs, birth certificates, and Social Security check stubs. The material allows users to piece together the life histories of individual Korean Americans, among them: Soon Hyun, an activist in the Korean resistance movement against Japanese colonialism in 1919, who later moved to the United States and became a minister in Hawaii; or Florence Ahn, a Korean American who became a prominent singer in Los Angeles. These personal biographies, in turn, allow users to examine the human dimension of the history of Asian Americans and their place as individuals within a larger history. *BP*

113. *Ling Long* Women's Magazine, Shanghai, 1931–1937

Columbia University Libraries

http://www.columbia.edu/cu/lweb/digital/collections/linglong/

Ling long, a weekly Chinese women's magazine published in Shanghai from 1931 to 1937, was popular during a time of sweeping social change in China. This website offers a nearly complete run of the magazine. Almost all of the text is in Chinese, but the abundance of graphic images, such as photographs, cartoons, and advertisements, makes this an important resource for studying urban mass culture and women's lives in 1930s Shanghai. Articles cover fashion, interior decorating, child-rearing, popular psychology, new careers, love, sex, and marriage. In addition, there are many illustrations of local women of "high society," young female authors, and American celebrities, such as movie stars and athletes. Advertisements for women's products also appear frequently. This is a valuable resource for studying Chinese social and cultural history as well as the globalization of culture, such as the rise of Hollywood as a global cultural influence, and the "modern girl" as a global phenomenon. *MC*

114. Mahatma Gandhi Research and Media Service

Gandhi Serve Foundation (Germany)

http://www.gandhiserve.org

Created to promote the life and teachings of Mohandas K. Gandhi, better known as Mahatma Gandhi, this website offers a vast collection of primary source mate-

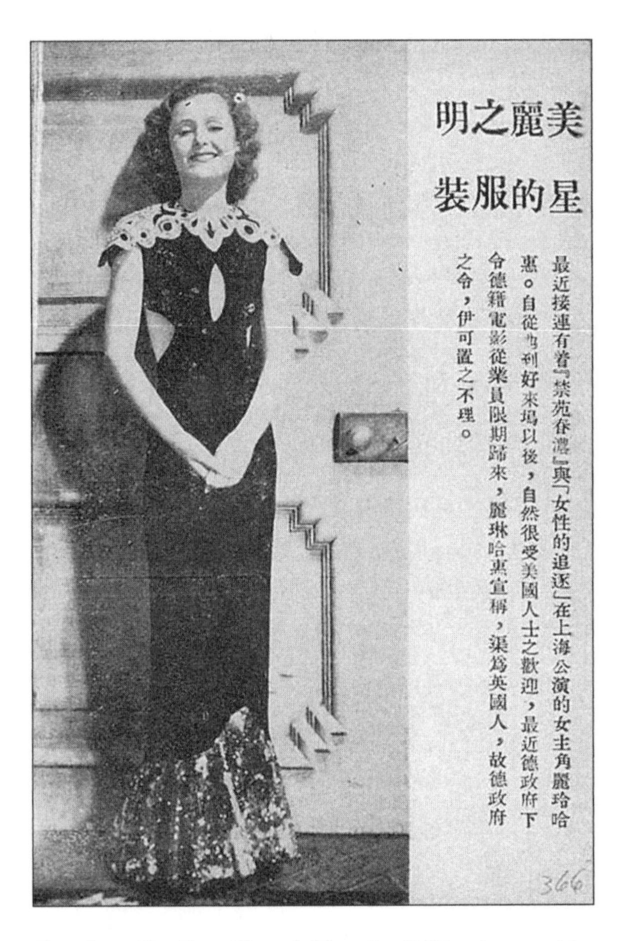

美麗之明星的服裝

最近接連有着『禁苑春濃』與「女性的追逐」在上海公演的女主角麗玲哈惠。自從她到好來塢以後，自然很受美國人士之歡迎，最近德政府下命德籍電影從業員限期歸來，麗琳哈惠宣稱，渠為英國人，故德政府之命，伊可置之不理。

Page from *Ling Long Women's Magazine* [113]. *(Courtesy of the C. V. Starr East Asian Library, Columbia University.)*

rials, including 15,000 photographs, six hours of documentary clips on Gandhi's life, 35,000 letters written to and by Gandhi, and 140 hours of audio clips (including more than ten hours of Gandhi's voice in English). For those new to Gandhi's legacy, the "Who's Gandhi?" essay offers an overview of his life and philosophy that places these materials in historical context. The "Online Image Archive" includes thousands of photographs, works of art, and political cartoons. Although some of this material makes very specific references to events in Gandhi's personal and political life, the images are an ideal way to become more familiar with the history of India, colonialism, and Gandhi himself. The website could use clearer organization and does advertise Gandhi-related materials, but the plentiful primary sources are free. *RD*

115. Marxists Internet Archive

Jorn Andersen, Brian Basgen, Chris Croome, Alphonso Pangas, David Walters, and a global volunteer cooperative

http://www.marxists.org

Marxist ideology has played a significant role in world history, especially in the twentieth century, and many of the sources found in this extensive archive are essential to a complete understanding of the Cold War and anti-colonial and liberation movements in the developing world. Materials include the work of more than 300 authors in thirty languages and tens of thousands of pages of text. An additional 500 images plus dozens of audio files makes this the most comprehensive library of Marxist thought available online. At the heart of the collection are the complete writings of Marx and Engels in English and Chinese. There are also large collections of works by Mao, Che Guevara, and Ho Chi Minh. Not all of the writers here are Marxists; Charles Darwin, for example, is included because his work influenced Marxist writers. The resources allow for interesting cross-cultural comparisons. For instance, users can examine how Asian Marxists described European colonialism as compared to how European or Latin American Marxists did. *TMK*

116. Material from the Antarctic Collections

State Library of New South Wales, Sydney, Australia

http://www.sl.nsw.gov.au/antarctica/

After Robert Scott's ill-fated attempt to reach the South Pole in 1910, Douglas Mawson mounted another expedition to Antarctica focused more exclusively on scientific investigation. Of great importance to that expedition's visual record was the inclusion of James "Frank" Hurley. Hurley established his formidable reputation as a still photographer and documentary filmmaker on this voyage to Antarctica, officially called the Australasian Antarctic Expedition (1911–1914). This website presents 100 photographs, twenty-five scientific drawings, and fifteen documents, as well as links to a database that contains the complete collection of images from the expedition — more than 2,000 in all. The materials record not only the activities of the members of the expedition party, including menus and celebration toast lists, but also their scientific findings, including drawings of the Aurora Polaris and maps of the party's route. Together, these materials are especially useful for exam-

Copper alloy weight depicting a porcupine from *National Museum of African Art* [117]. *(Weight, Akan peoples, Côte d'Ivoire, Ghana, 8th–19th century, Copper alloy, 1⅞ x 1½ x 3 in. Gift of Philip L. Ravenhill in memory of Sylvia H. Williams. 96-42-3. Photograph by Franko Khoury, National Museum of African Art, Smithsonian Institution.)*

ining exploration, discovery, and scientific endeavor more broadly, as well as early twentieth-century photography. *KM*

117. National Museum of African Art

Smithsonian Institution

http://www.nmafa.si.edu/index2.html

African art and culture can be explored through this website with a central focus on artwork from across the African continent. Materials include more than 1,500 ancient artifacts, pieces collected in the colonial era, photographs, textiles, and works by modern African artists. The "Collections" section allows users to locate art by country, kind of imagery, ethnic group, material, motif, function, or artist. The "Arts and Programs" section provides forty virtual exhibitions that help provide context. For example, the exhibition "A Spiral of History: A Carved Tusk from the Loango Coast, Congo," showcases a carved ivory tusk from late nineteenth-century Congo. Objects such as *nkisi* power figures from the Kongo peoples, carved female cult figures, photographs, hats, and much more can be used to examine common motifs in the art and gain a wider understanding of the history and culture of this part of Africa. *AG*

118. Native American Constitution and Law Digitization Project

University of Oklahoma Law Library and the National Indian Law Library

http://thorpe.ou.edu/

This website presents full-text versions of 500 codes, constitutions, treaties, land titles, and Supreme Court decisions relating to the more than 500 Native American tribes in the United States. The bulk of the material lies in the "IRA (Indian Reorganization Act) Era Constitutions and Charters" section that offers close to 300 documents: primarily corporate charters, constitutions, and bylaws from the 1930s and 1940s. The website also includes the 1936 Composite Indian Reorganization Act for Alaska, and twentieth-century constitutions from selected tribes, such as the Choctaw Nation of Oklahoma. For material before the twentieth century, the "Treaties" section includes scans of the original Six Nations Treaty of 1794 and the Senekas Treaties of 1797 and 1823. In addition, a digitized version of Felix Cohen's 1941 *Handbook of Federal Indian Law*, and the *Opinions of the Solicitor of the Department of the Interior Relating to Indian Affairs 1917–1974* are both available. *KDL*

Photograph of aboriginal children from *PictureAustralia* [119].
(Photographer, Lyn McLeavy.)

119. PictureAustralia

National Library of Australia
http://www.pictureaustralia.org/

Antarctic exploration, changing kitchen technologies, and the *Ballets Russes* represent only three of the many topics accessible through this vast collection of 600,000 images documenting Australia's cultural history. The collection includes photographs, artwork (such as paintings, drawings, prints, and posters), and objects that range in time period from seventeenth-century voyages of European expansion to the present day. Items can be located through a simple search from the homepage, or through an advanced search using a variety of categories. Searches by subject allow images from the Pacific region to be incorporated into studies of world history in a thematic way, from European encounters with indigenous peoples to the Pacific as a site of war. The clear reproduction of "Black-eyed Sue and Sweet Poll of Plymouth taking leave of their lovers who are going to Botany Bay," for example, illuminates popular representations of transportation as well as images of women, criminals, and the poor at the end of the eighteenth century. *KM*

120. Reverend Claude L. Pickens Collection on Muslims in China

Raymond Lum, Harvard-Yenching Library, Harvard University
http://hcl.harvard.edu/libraries/harvard-yenching/collections/pickens/

Reverend Claude L. Pickens (1900–1985), an American missionary who was affiliated with the China Inland Mission (C.I.M.), recorded many of his experiences with a camera. This website presents 1,000 black-and-white photographs taken by Pickens of Chinese Muslims (now officially categorized as "Hui") as well as of Christian missionaries working among them. Although China remained politically fragmented in the 1930s, a nascent Nationalist (Guomindang) state headed by Generalissimo Chiang Kai-shek and based in Nanjing (Nanking), was attempting to implement programs of modernization, mostly in large urban centers. Against this backdrop, the collection documents both the work of the C.I.M. missionaries and the daily life, architecture, and religious practices of the various Muslim communities with whom they came into contact. To locate these images, click on the "View the Photographs in the VIA Catalogue" link, enter "Claude L. Pickens" in the "Name" field, check the box limiting the search to records with digital images, and select the "Harvard-Yenching Library" in the "Limit repository to:" field. These photographs provide a way to explore remote areas and communities of China during the 1930s. *MC*

121. SouthEast Asian Images and Texts

University of Wisconsin Digital Collections
http://digicoll.library.wisc.edu/SEAiT/About.html

The Philippines and Laos are the focus of this collection of primary and secondary resources, including more than 3,600 high-quality photographs. The 630 images from the Philippines date primarily from the early 1900s, although several were taken as late as the 1940s. The subjects of these photographs range from images of war, religion, workplaces, and street scenes to general depictions of daily life. The more than 3,000 photographs dealing with Laos were complied largely through the work of Joel M. Halpern, a professor of anthropology in the 1950s and 1960s. These primarily depict regional ethnic groups, Buddhist monks, temples, and celebrations. In addition, there are nine short scholarly articles by historian Alfred W. McCoy, all grouped under the heading "Orientalism of the Philippine Photograph: America Discovers the Philippine Islands." Each image is meticulously cataloged and labeled, making the collection useful for examining many subjects, including military topics, family life, and U.S. imperialism in the region. *RD*

122. *The Stars and Stripes*: The American Soldiers' Newspaper of World War I, 1918–19

Library of Congress, American Memory Project
http://memory.loc.gov/ammem/sgphtml/sashtml/sashome.html

From February 1918 to June 1919, the United States Army published a weekly newspaper, *The Stars and Stripes*, for its forces in France. The newspaper regularly featured American news, sports, poetry, and cartoons, and was designed to provide troops scattered across the Western Front — and often embedded among Italian, French, and British forces — with a sense of unity and purpose. This website has digitized complete editions of all seventy-one issues of the paper, which offer users the opportunity to experience firsthand how American soldiers conceived of (and were taught to conceive of) their interactions with soldiers from other countries. In addition, many articles address not only political and current events, but also topics such as food and etiquette that provide a glimpse into the daily lives of American soldiers. The website includes a map of the American forces in Europe for context. Though the newspapers are sometimes slow to load, all issues are keyword searchable and can be zoomed for detailed viewing. *KDL*

123. Timeframes

National Library of New Zealand
http://timeframes.natlib.govt.nz/

This collection of more than 21,000 images specializes in the social and natural history of New Zealand, the Pacific, and Antarctica from the beginning of European contact to the present. Some subject headings are particularly helpful for comparative work or for studying world history in a thematic way, such as "World War, 1939–1945" or "Trade Unions." The browse feature also includes lesser-known subjects such as "Afternoon tea," which presents a series of images that speak to the colonial use of space and landscape through social rituals. These images could be analyzed across diverse examples of transplanted cultures on a global scale. Although the lack of editorial guidance through the large collection is a drawback, a recent publication could add some contextualization. *A History of Australia, New Zealand and the Pacific* by Donald Denoon et al. presents the history of New Zealand thematically, connecting it to broader trends within the surrounding region. KM

124. United States Holocaust Memorial Museum

United States Holocaust Memorial Museum

http://www.ushmm.org/

Though a visit to this website cannot replace the sobering experience of visiting the museum in person, it does provide widespread access to the museum's vast archival collections and educational resources. A general introduction to the Holocaust is provided in the "History" section, including brief articles on victims, refugees, the camp system, anti-Semitism, and the Final Solution. There are also links to more than fifty online exhibits. For example, "Tracing Their Fate: St. Louis Passengers" provides information about the *S.S. St. Louis*, a ship loaded with passengers seeking asylum from Germany in 1939 that was rejected at ports in Cuba and the U.S. Other exhibits focus on the Warsaw Ghetto uprising, *Kristallnacht*, Oskar Schindler, Anne Frank, and American responses to the Holocaust. The "Education" section

Diary from nine-year-old Peter Feigl in the *United States Holocaust Memorial Museum* [124]. *(Permission of The United States Holocaust Memorial Museum.)*

includes online activities for students. The "Research" section furnishes links to the museum's collections, library, and survivors registry. Finally, the "Conscience" section highlights regions, like Sudan and Chechnya, that are currently faced with genocide, providing information useful for contemporary comparisons. *WH*

125. Virtual Shanghai: Shanghai Urban Space in Time

Institute of East Asian Studies, Center for Chinese Studies, and Electronic Cultural Atlas Initiative

http://virtualshanghai.net

These 3,000 photographic images, 250 maps, and ten texts focus on Shanghai from the nineteenth century through the mid-twentieth century, presenting a wealth of visual material about this busy port city. The collection is heavily oriented toward themes of urban planning and architecture, and is strongest in presenting images of traffic, gardens, factories, workers, advertisements, shops, entertainment, school campuses, soldiers, clothing and uniforms, and modes of transport, such as bicycles, rickshaws, railways, steamboats, and automobiles. One of the most unique aspects of this collection is the visual documentation of the Japanese assault on the city in 1932, one of the earliest aerial bombardment campaigns of the Pacific war. The images documenting education in Shanghai are particularly interesting, showing campuses (mostly located in the foreign sections), portraits of (mostly foreign) instructors, and sporting events, though there is a clear predilection for photographers to document the foreign impact and presence within this semi-colonial city. *MC*

126. World War I Document Archive

Great War Primary Documents Archive, Inc.

http://net.lib.byu.edu/~rdh7/wwi/

Hundreds of primary-source documents and images from all over the world relating to World War I, with particular emphasis on the military, diplomatic, and political dimensions of the war, are presented on this website. Government documents are arranged both chronologically and by type, including treaties and convention proceedings from sixteen countries. Additional documents include information about the maritime war and the medical front as well as seventy-five personal reminiscences, such as diaries, books, letters, and poems. There are two image collections. One provides 1,844 images divided into fifteen categories, including heads of state, refugees, and locations, such as battlefields and camps. Another provides thumbnail photographs and descriptions of medals divided by country. The website also offers full-text versions of more than fifty recent books, several of which highlight Chinese and Japanese participation in the war, and a World War I biographical dictionary of more than 200 prominent people. *KDL*

More Related Websites

Africa Focus: Sights and Sounds of a Continent [127]

Africa Online Digital Library [128]

African National Congress, Historical Documents Archive [129]

American Family Immigration History Center [70]

Australian Studies Resources [72]
BBC Audio Interviews [131]
COLLAGE [73]
Collect Britain [5]
Collections Canada [74]
David Rumsey Collection [75]
Decision to Drop the Atomic Bomb [136]
Digital South Asia Library [6]
Early Canadiana Online [76]
Famous Trials [8]
Foreign Relations of the United States [138]
From History to Herstory: Yorkshire Women's Lives Online, 1100 to the Present [79]
Gertrude Bell Project [80]
Getty Digitized Library Collections [9]
Gifts of Speech: Women's Speeches from Around the World [140]
Harappa: The Indus Valley and the Raj in India and Pakistan [81]
Historical Maps, Perry-Castañada Library Map Collection [82]
In Motion: The African-American Migration Experience [83]
Kyoto National Museum [13]
Mexico: From Empire to Revolution [89]
Mysteries in Canadian History [90]
National Security Archive [142]
Oxford Latin American Economic History Database [143]
Pauline Johnson Archive [91]
Political Database of the Americas [144]
Seventeen Moments in Soviet History [146]
South Texas Border, 1900–1920: Photographs from the Robert Runyon Collection [94]
Thinker ImageBase [15]
Tibetan and Himalayan Digital Library [147]
Uysal-Walker Archive of Turkish Oral Narrative [149]
Visual Arts Data Services [150]
Women's Library: Suffrage Banners Collection [97]
Women's Travel Writing, 1830–1930: Women's Studies Digitization Project [98]

Promises and Paradoxes: The World Since 1945

127. Africa Focus: Sights and Sounds of a Continent

University of Wisconsin-Madison Libraries

http://africafocus.library.wisc.edu

This large collection of primary sources in African studies includes more than 3,500 images, fifty hours of sound, and seven digitized texts, four of which are extremely rare. The digitized texts include translations of sixteenth- and seventeenth-century European accounts of Africa, two bibliographies, and a recent (1986) edited volume on slavery. The website's main focus is the "Image and Audio Collection," divided into topic categories: "Drums," "Greetings," "Rites and Ceremonies," "Songs and Singing," "Artisans," "Buildings and Structures," "Cities," and "Women." Detailed source information allows for fruitful browsing and searching. For example, a keyword search on "pastoralism" — a nomadic or semi-nomadic way of life, centered around herding animals — allows users to see how widespread this way of life is across the African continent, and to gain insight into what this life entails among specific ethnic groups, such as the Nuer of Sudan. *AG*

128. Africa Online Digital Library

MATRIX: Center for Humane Arts, Letters and Social Sciences Online, Michigan State University

http://www.aodl.org/

The materials on this site on a variety of topics in African history come mainly from West Africa. Primary sources are divided into seven galleries, including more than 500 images, texts, and sound files. There are close to 400 high-quality photographs — taken primarily by historian Philip Curtin in the 1960s — that show a broad spectrum of West African social, economic, and artistic life. A more thematically-driven collection holds about fifty photographs that represent the urban visual culture of the Mourides, a Senegalese Sufi movement. A smaller collection contains eighteen photographs of mosques in Bondoukou, located in eastern Cote d'Ivoire. A collection of text documents from HIV/AIDS conferences, collected by West African researcher Charles Becker, dates from the early 1980s and charts the study of the pandemic in Africa. Finally, the "Fuuta Tooro Oral History Project" contains sound files from three interviews conducted by noted historian David Robinson in the 1960s. Taken together, these resources are useful for both a close examination of select topics in African history, and for teaching Africa in global perspective. *EAP*

129. African National Congress, Historical Documents Archive

The African National Congress

http://www.anc.org.za/ancdocs/history/

This archive contains hundreds of speeches by African National Congress (ANC) leaders, as well as press releases, conference proceedings, and articles and pamphlets tracing the development of this leading South African liberation organization from its origins in 1912 to the present. Many of the writings not only chart policies over the past century, but also highlight strategies that succeeding generations of activists tailored to suit changing political environments. There are no bells and whistles, yet the compelling writings from ANC stalwarts (such as Albert Lutuli, Oliver Tambo, and Nelson Mandela), as well as activists from other liberation fronts, need no enhancement. An impressive search engine enables users to locate materials by person (from foot soldier and protestor to path-breaker); event (*e.g.*, the treason trials and major boycotts); white supremacist legislation (*e.g.*, racial pass laws and States of Emergency); international links (*e.g.*, the anti-apartheid movement and United Nations initiatives); and affiliated organizations (*e.g.*, United Democratic Front and Congress of South African Trade Unions). One can supplement these documents by consulting *From Protest to Challenge* by Thomas Karis and Gwendoline M. Carter (eds.) (1972–1977, 4 vols.), a collection of essays on the anti-apartheid movement. *BC, RE*

130. African Posters

Melville J. Herskovitz Library, Northwestern University

http://www.library.northwestern.edu/africana/collections/posters/index.html

This website presents more than 350 posters, focusing primarily on South Africa and the struggle against apartheid, with good representation of anti-colonial struggles in Portuguese Africa as well. Many posters include artwork or photographs as well as text; many are in color and a few are multilingual. Posters focus on well-known leaders, organizations, and events of the anti-apartheid struggle, such as Nelson Mandela, the African National Congress (ANC), Stephen (Steve) Biko, the Sharpeville massacre, and the 1976 Soweto student uprising. One theme that emerges is the international quality of the anti-apartheid movement. Some posters represent specific elements of the international campaign to pressure the South African government through arms and sports boycotts as well as trade and financial sanctions, including divestment. The collection also offers an opportunity to explore themes that unify anti-colonial and other struggles worldwide, and African history and politics, human rights, and international and contemporary history more generally. *EAP*

131. BBC Audio Interviews

British Broadcasting Corporation

http://www.bbc.co.uk/bbcfour/audiointerviews/

Since its inception in 1922, the British Broadcasting Corporation (BBC) has interviewed thousands of leading political, literary, religious, cultural, and academic figures. This archive presents more than 150 of these audio and video interviews. Most interviewees are European and American, but a sizable number of notables from around the world are represented, including Salman Rushdie, Chinua Achebe, Nadine Gordimer, Gandhi, the Dalai Lama, Desmond Tutu, and Ravi Shankar. Most interviews occurred in the 1980s or 1990s, though a few interviews are from the 1960s and 1970s. Many interviewees, however, describe influential events from the 1930s and 1940s. Brief profiles of all interviewees are available, and additional web resources, such as BBC profiles, articles, or obituaries are available for most. *KDL*

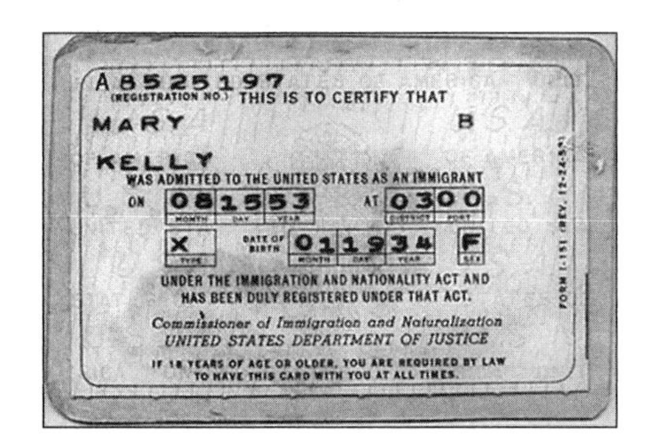
A8525197
(REGISTRATION NO.) THIS IS TO CERTIFY THAT
MARY B
KELLY
WAS ADMITTED TO THE UNITED STATES AS AN IMMIGRANT
ON 08 15 53 AT 0300
X DATE OF BIRTH 01 19 34 F
UNDER THE IMMIGRATION AND NATIONALITY ACT AND
HAS BEEN DULY REGISTERED UNDER THAT ACT.
Commissioner of Immigration and Naturalization
UNITED STATES DEPARTMENT OF JUSTICE
IF 18 YEARS OF AGE OR OLDER, YOU ARE REQUIRED BY LAW
TO HAVE THIS CARD WITH YOU AT ALL TIMES.

Registration card from *Breaking the Silence* [132]. *(Copyright, Irish Centre for Migration Studies, University College Cork, Ireland.)*

132. Breaking the Silence

Irish Centre for Migration Studies
http://migration.ucc.ie/oralarchive/testing/breaking/index.html

In the 1950s, Ireland experienced a period of heavy emigration — its heaviest in the twentieth century. This oral history project collected seventy-eight oral and twelve written life histories from Irish men and women focused on the decision to emigrate or remain in Ireland. The people interviewed represent a broad spectrum of Irish life, but were all born between 1910 and 1940. The majority are non-emigrants, though virtually all speak of family members or close friends who chose to emigrate. The oral histories, which range in length from twelve minutes to more than three hours, are available as streaming audio, and are described in detail — helpful when searching for specific information. To contextualize these life histories, the website includes thirty newspaper clippings, poems, and songs, more than 500 photographs of daily life, and official statistics on emigration. These sources highlight prominent themes surrounding Ireland's demographic crisis in the 1950s, including modernization and changes in traditional ways of life. *KDL*

133. Cambodian Genocide Program

Yale University Genocide Studies Program
http://www.yale.edu/cgp/

Between 1975 and 1979, the Khmer Rouge, under the direction of Communist leader Pol Pot, murdered roughly twenty-one percent of the Cambodian population (1.3 million people). This website provides rare and informative resources related to this terrible period in human history, including more than fifty maps, seventy-five bibliographic references, and four online databases, which contain thousands of entries of biographic information (including interviews with survivors) not preserved elsewhere. More than 10,000 photographs of those who were systematically imprisoned, tortured, and killed by the Khmer Rouge are searchable by various categories, including gender, age, and clothing. Photographs of the Choeung Ek killing fields and the infamous grade school that was transformed into a gruesome prison, known as Tuol Sleng or "S-21," are also available. When coupled with the biographical information and interviews, these materials provide a grim and poignant reminder of the individual tragedies that underlie the staggering statistics associated with these crimes. *RD*

134. Castro Speech Database

Latin American Network Information Center, University of Texas
http://lanic.utexas.edu/la/cb/cuba/castro.html

After the overthrow of General Fulgencio Batista's regime in Cuba in 1959, Communist party leader Fidel Castro assumed power and remained the head of state into the twenty-first century. This collection contains English translations of thousands of Castro's speeches, interviews, and press conferences given between 1959 and 1996, providing substantial material for studying the Cuban Revolution and the subsequent decades. While many speeches are presented in their entirety, others are paraphrased. Beware: secondhand accounts of Castro's speeches are often quite superficial. Nevertheless, the collection is extensive and fully searchable. A search for "Che Guevara" allows users to explore Castro's symbolic use of this legendary Marxist revolutionary. Zeroing in on a specific moment in the revolutionary period (the "Push to Communism" of the late 1960s or the "Special Period" after the fall of the Soviet Union) is also possible. Finally, searches with keywords, such as "democracy," "women," "blacks," and "religion" illuminate Castro's thinking on certain crucial topics in the history of the Revolution. *MK*

135. Chinese Propaganda Posters

Stefan Landsberger, Leiden University, The Netherlands
http://www.iisg.nl/~landsberger/

These propaganda posters represent many facets of Chinese political, social, and economic life. Many of the hundreds of posters available on this website are from 1970 or later, but the entire collection spans five decades. Posters are organized according to subject matter and/or historical periods or events. These include: "Early Campaigns (1950s)," the "Great Leap Forward," "Models and Martyrs," "Heroes and Villains," "Party and State Leaders," the "People's Liberation Army," "National Minorities," the "Mao Cult," "Cultural Revolution Campaigns," "Environment," and "Population Policy" as well as current events, such as the "Fifth National Census, 2000" and the "Beijing Olympics 2008." In addition to cross-cultural and historical comparisons, these images provide a window into the aspirations and

Poster from *Chinese Propaganda Posters* [135]. *(Courtesy of IISH Stefan R. Landsberger Collection, image numbers G02/029 and G02/030, http://www.iisg.nl/~landsberger.)*

ideals (a certain brand of women's liberation, land and wealth redistribution, general social justice) that inspired China's socialist revolution and led to the successes (and failures) of the Chinese Communist Party. *MC*

136. Decision to Drop the Atomic Bomb

Truman Presidential Museum and Library

http://www.trumanlibrary.org/whistlestop/study_collections/bomb/large/index.php

The most significant and controversial act of American president Harry Truman was the dropping of the atomic bombs on the Japanese cities of Hiroshima and Nagasaki in August 1945. This website explores that decision through a collection of 100 documents, including many documents that scholars use when debating the necessity or morality of the bombing, such as minutes from important meetings and memos from Truman's key advisers. Although the website contains several documents often used by scholars who are critical of Truman and his motivation, there is no forum for critical views on the bombing of Hiroshima and Nagasaki. Indeed, upon examining the website, users unfamiliar with the topic would have little idea that it addresses what is arguably the most controversial decision of the twentieth century. The website should, therefore, be used in conjunction with other materials. A short, balanced, and accessible book is J. Samuel Walker's *Prompt and Utter Destruction* (1997). *BP*

137. Digital Imaging Project of South Africa

University of Natal

http://disa.nu.ac.za/

The years between 1960 and 1994 were pivotal in South Africa's liberation struggle. The white minority that controlled the apartheid government created sophisticated mechanisms to suppress dissent, especially in the early 1960s. Anti-apartheid organizations, however, continued to disseminate their message through newsletters, pamphlets, bulletins, and newspapers. This collection presents multiple issues from forty-three anti-apartheid periodicals, starting in 1950. Together, the materials offer competing perspectives, both political and nonpolitical. For example, the African National Congress (ANC) and its allies (*African Communist*, *Dawn*, *Isizwe*) favored non-racialism. Other groups wanted to mobilize Africans and exclude whites. In the

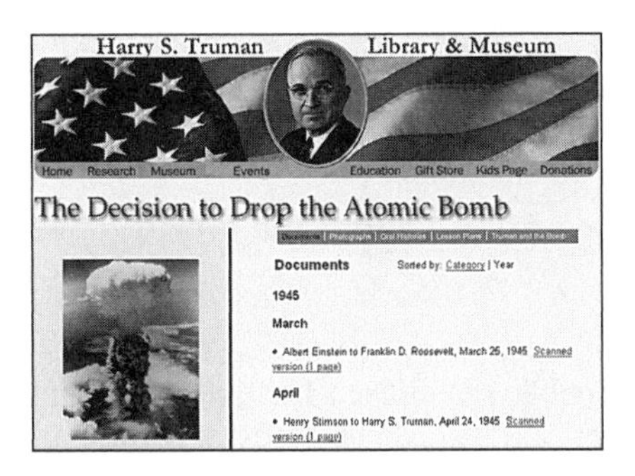

Screenshot from *Decision to Drop the Atomic Bomb* [136]. *(The Harry S. Truman Library.)*

1970s, an ascendant Black Consciousness movement (*Black Review*, *Frank Talk*) redefined what it meant to be black, including all people targeted for oppression by apartheid laws. By showing how broader freedoms are won through a variety of political approaches, these periodicals demonstrate that the fabric of multiracial democracy contains a patchwork of dissenting views. *BC, RE*

138. Foreign Relations of the United States

U.S. Department of State, Office of the Historian
http://www.state.gov/r/pa/ho/frus/

This official archive of the U.S. State Department presents the documentary history (official reports, correspondence, and transcriptions of Presidential tape recordings) of major U.S. foreign policy decisions from the Truman, Eisenhower, Kennedy, Johnson, and Nixon-Ford administrations. Together, these materials provide examples of both formal and informal statements of diplomacy. The bulk of the material covers the Kennedy and Johnson administrations, with special emphasis on Israel, Egypt, and Iran. These documents provide evidence of the attitudes American diplomats and officials held toward the Middle East and address foreign relations from an American perspective at the height of the Cold War. Other prominent topics include the Vietnam War, Cuba and the Cuban Missile Crisis, foreign economic policy, China, and the Soviet Union. Pairing these documents with media reports would allow for an interesting examination of the parallels and disparities between public awareness and government considerations in the construction of foreign policy. *NS, KDL*

139. GenderStats

The World Bank Gender and Development Group
http://devdata.worldbank.org/genderstats/

Designed primarily for users with development agency backgrounds, this set of data relating to gender issues from more than 200 countries is also useful for studying world history in the late twentieth century in a number of ways. The data are organized by country, theme, region, and specific category, such as "Education," "Opportunity," and "Empowerment." These categories allow users to investigate change over time in the relative position of men and women in society, make regional comparisons, and chart government intervention in gender issues. The data cover a sufficiently long period so one can fruitfully explore the degree to which a change in government or political system (such as the demise of apartheid in South Africa) brings changes in gender demographics. This dataset also opens an avenue for discussion about the collection and interpretation of statistics on gender issues and the production of knowledge more generally. *KM*

140. Gifts of Speech: Women's Speeches from Around the World

Sweet Briar College, Virginia
http://www.giftsofspeech.org

Charting changes in women's rhetoric in the public realm from 1800 to the present is possible through this archive of speeches by "influential, contemporary women," including prominent female politicians and scientists, as well as popular culture figures. While there is an emphasis on the United States (particularly after 1900) the collection is global in its reach, including speeches from women as diverse as Human Rights Activist Constance Yai or Charlotte van Rappard-Boon of the Netherlands Ministry of Education, Culture, and Science. A nearly complete list of "Nobel Lectures by Women Laureates" would provide a particular theme to follow in investigating women's public rhetoric. The search function is particularly useful for pulling speeches from a diverse collection into common subject groups. It also allows for the study of the language of women's public debate by following changes in the use of particular metaphors or idioms, such as the use of the concept "motherhood." *KM*

141. Morning Sun

Long Bow Group
http://www.morningsun.org/

Designed to accompany a two-hour documentary on China's Cultural Revolution (ca. 1964–1976) entitled "Morning Sun" (Fall 2003), this website provides an introduction to "the psycho-emotional topography of high-Maoist China." One goal is to understand the powerful effect of revolutionary ideals and perhaps ideological rhetoric in general. The website is divided into thematic categories that tell the history of the Cultural Revolution: "Living the Revolution," "Smash the Old World," "Reddest Red Sun," "Stages of History," and "The East is Red." Additional materials include films and music; more than 100 images, such as photographs and artwork; and more than twenty primary and secondary texts. These sources are especially useful for studying the relationship between politics, mass mobilization, and mass media. The creators of the website also raise issues of the difference between moral judgment and historical understanding when confronting the past. *MC*

142. National Security Archive

National Security Archive, George Washington University
http://www.gwu.edu/~nsarchiv/

This archive is dedicated to making available U.S. documents declassified by the Freedom of Information Act. In fulfilling this mission, it contains hundreds of government documents, primarily collected in briefing books that include detailed scholarly introductions and an annotated collection of primary sources. These materials offer the chance to explore the difficult nature of policymaking that is often shaped by pre-existing attitudes and incomplete intelligence. Holdings on Latin America and Europe are particularly strong. The documents were produced by the U.S. government, but they often shed light on local events, such as the forty-eight documents included in the briefing book, "The Guatemalan Military: What the U.S. Files Reveal," which provides an illuminating look at the structure and behavior of that institution during Guatemala's decades-long civil war. It is important to note that the archive's materials have been selected carefully by the National Security Archive, whose aim is to blow the whistle on U.S. malfeasance. Still, the Archive is hardly an extremist organization, and its interpretations are generally reasonable. *WH, MK, KDL*

143. Oxford Latin American Economic History Database

Latin American Centre, Oxford University

http://oxlad.qeh.ox.ac.uk/

This database contains a wealth of statistical information on Latin American economies and societies in an easily searchable format, focusing specifically on demographic, social, and economic statistics of twenty countries from 1900 to 2000. Data are available on population and demographics, the labor force, trade, industry, transportation and communications, tax revenue, government spending, and prices. To access data, users select a country or countries, specify the date range, and select a statistical series. A click of the mouse produces an easy-to-read chart that can be viewed on-screen, printed, or downloaded as a CSV (comma separated value) file. Used wisely, this website can serve as an introduction to Latin American economic history and to the practice of interpreting statistics. Analyzing data on GDP, life expectancy, illiteracy, and education spending from various countries should reveal the heterogeneity of Latin America, while allowing users to probe the extent to which various countries have prioritized social spending in different periods. *MK*

144. Political Database of the Americas

Georgetown University

http://pdba.georgetown.edu/

The extensive primary documents, statistical data, and reference materials collected here cover the governmental structures of thirty-five countries in the Western Hemisphere. Though the website is hosted in the United States, the U.S. receives no more attention than do countries in Latin America and the Caribbean. The materials are divided by theme and are searchable by country within each theme, including: "Constitutions and Comparative Constitutional Study," "Executive Branch," "Legislative Branch," "Judicial Branch," "Electoral Systems and Election Data," "Political Parties," "Decentralization and Local Governance," "Democracy and Citizen Security," "Indigenous Peoples," and "Civil Society." A keyword search is also available. This structure fosters comparisons — for example, of governmental structure, political party make-up, or election results — across countries. While the website text is in English, one potential drawback is that much of the primary-source material is available only in the language in which it was written. *KDL*

145. *Red-Color News Soldier* — Li Zhensheng: A Chinese Photographer's Odyssey Through the Cultural Revolution

Robert Pledge, Contact Press Images

http://red-colornewssoldier.com/

Li Zhensheng (b. 1940), a Chinese photojournalist based in Heilongjiang province, participated in and recorded China's "Great Proletarian Cultural Revolution" (GPCR, 1966–1976). These thirty photographs (five self-portraits and twenty-five scenes from the GPCR in China's Heilongjiang province) are selections from a more comprehensive, 300-page companion volume also entitled *Red-Color News Soldier*. Li Zhensheng's personality and sense of historical mission are readily apparent; indeed, they seem to be the necessary precondition for the preservation and publication of this stunning and unique collection of "negative negatives" documenting one of the most momentous and perplexing episodes not only in Chinese history, but in the twentieth century more generally. The Cultural Revolution makes a wonderful case study of how ideological rhetoric — when espoused, disseminated, and thus legitimated by those who wield power — can take on a life of its own. *MC*

146. Seventeen Moments in Soviet History

James von Geldern and Lewis Siegelbaum

http://www.soviethistory.org/

From its creation in the Russian Revolution of 1917 to its collapse under Mikhail Gorbachev in 1991, the communist enterprise in the Soviet Union sought the radical and complete transformation of all aspects of life — from social relations to the economy, from everyday life to nature itself. These changes manifested themselves in vastly different forms over time. This website traces these changes along a timeline of "Seventeen Moments" demarcated by individual years in Soviet history. It features well-known events, such as Nikita Khrushchev's "Secret Speech" denouncing Stalin's crimes in 1956, and lesser-known events such as the construction of the Great Fergana Canal in Uzbekistan in 1939. Extensive introductory essays, hundreds of audio and video clips of famous songs and films, thousands of archival documents and published sources translated into English, and hundreds of other visual media such as paintings and posters illuminate these "moments" and allow users to contextualize them in relation to other social, political, economic, and cultural developments. A free registration is required to access some of the resources. *SH*

147. Tibetan and Himalayan Digital Library

Professor David Germano, University of Virginia

http://www.thdl.org/

This large collection of primary source materials sheds light on the environment, culture, and history of Tibet and the Himalayas. The "Collections" section contains the bulk of the primary materials and is subdivided into "Images," "Audio/Video," "Maps," "Texts," "Journals," and thematic sections such as "Religion," "Art," "Literature," "Medicine," and "Architecture," which includes an interactive ground plan of the Sera Monastery, an important Tibetan monastic educational institution dating from the fifteenth century. There is also a three-dimensional reconstruction of the Meru Nyingba monastery that can be useful in trying to visualize the architectural form of the structure. While many Tibetan texts are not translated, users can see portions of a Tibetan palm leaf manuscript or large passages of Tibetan texts as well as many other images. *RD*

148. Trust Territory Photo Archives

University of Hawaii

http://libweb.hawaii.edu/digicoll/ttp/ttpi.html

The Trust Territory of the Pacific Islands comprises three major Micronesian archipelagoes in the Pacific Ocean that came under the control of the United States as a United Nations strategic trusteeship following World War II. The Trust Territory is

Photograph of a man and child in Agrihan from *Trust Territory Photo Archives* [148]. *(Photo provided by Bill Wedertz, United States Naval Academy. Trust Territory Archives, Pacific Collection, University of Hawaii Library.)*

unusual because the transitional arrangement remained in effect until 1990 and the territories remain strongly tied to the United States. This website presents more than 6,000 images that document the American period in Micronesia between 1947 and 1988. The photographs, primarily taken by people employed by the government or closely associated with it, provide an extensive record of American views of Micronesian peoples, society, and culture. The collection is extremely diverse, and covers themes including parades, dancing, health, architecture, and children. All images contain brief descriptions that are keyword searchable. This website provides an extensive visual record of cultural contact in a situation of quasi-colonialism that continued throughout much of the twentieth century. KM

149. Uysal-Walker Archive of Turkish Oral Narrative

Texas Tech University, Special Collections Library

http://aton.ttu.edu/

Over the past forty years, researchers at Texas Tech University collected thousands of Turkish folktales through interviews with several hundred Turks. This website presents English translations of these folktales (as PDF files), preserving oral traditions that might otherwise have been lost in a dynamic, twenty-first-century Turkey. The folktales are accompanied by hundreds of additional primary and secondary sources. More than forty topics in the "Guides" section contextualize the folktales, ranging from original Turkish publications of folktales to secondary accounts of the historical value of such literature in Turkey. Additional resources include 100 stories and poems, three audio files of readings, 100 audio files (MP3) of Turkish folk music, as well as lyric sheets for many songs, and close to 100 images of Turkish landmarks. As an added bonus, these materials also present the opportunity to study the Karagoz puppet tradition, a representation of Ottoman popular culture. *NS*

150. Visual Arts Data Services

Surrey Institute of Art and Design, University College
http://vads.ahds.ac.uk/collections/index.html

Thirty-six separate image collections form the core of this extensive website dedicated to enhancing art education. Many collections focus on the history of England (especially London), and are particularly strong on twentieth-century material culture, such as ceramics, fashion, textiles, and crafts, as well as architecture and design. For world history more broadly, the "African and Asian Visual Artists Archive" makes available more than 2,000 contemporary prints, paintings, and photographs by artists of African and Asian descent working in the U.K. The "Spanish Civil War Poster Collection" contains eighty-five posters related to that conflict, with examples of both Republican and Nationalist views concerning recruitment, propaganda, and agriculture. "Posters of Conflict" provides more than 2,000 posters and prints related to Britain's involvement in twentieth-century wars. Images are accessible through a combined "Search" page. Once there, click "Uncheck-all" and select only the collection(s) of interest. A browse function is not available, so users may want to reference books on specific topics for search words. *KDL*

More Related Websites

Ahlul-Bayt Digital Islamic Library Project [31]

Australian War Memorial [102]

Avalon Project: Documents in Law, History and Diplomacy [4]

Canadian Letters and Images Project [105]

COLLAGE [73]

Collections Canada [74]

Democracy at War: Canadian Newspapers and the Second World War [106]

Famous Trials [8]

From History to Herstory: Yorkshire Women's Lives Online, 1100 to the Present [79]

Frontera Collection of Mexican American Music [108]

Huntington Archive of Buddhist and Related Art [10]

In Motion: The African-American Migration Experience [83]

Korean American Digital Archive [112]

Kyoto National Museum [13]

Mahatma Gandhi Research and Media Service [114]

Marxists Internet Archive [115]

A Glossary of Common Internet Terms

A more extensive glossary may be found at: **http://www.matisse.net/files/glossary.html.**

Attachment: A document, photo, or other file that is sent via electronic mail. Users can download the attachment to read or view it. A writing assignment, for example, can be sent as an attachment.

Blog: (*short for* **Weblog**) A website that contains periodic, reverse chronologically ordered posts on a common webpage. Such a website is accessible to any Internet user. Individual posts (which taken together are the blog or weblog) either share a particular theme, or a single or small group of authors.

Bookmark: (*also* **Favorite**) A browser function that "saves" a website's location for easy return later on.

Broadband: Refers to the method by which data are transmitted to your computer. Communication via DSL, an Ethernet line, or a cable is considered broadband, as compared to transmission over a standard telephone line, which is not. Broadband transmissions can process more data in a shorter amount of time than telephone lines.

Browser: *See* **Web Browser.**

Chat: Synchronous communication between computers on the Internet using voice, video, or plain text. Common chat interfaces include Yahoo! Messenger, IRC, AIM, and Windows Messenger.

Cookie: (*also called* **HTTP Cookie**) A packet of information sent by a server to a browser and then sent back by the browser each time it accesses that server. Typically this is used to authenticate or identify a registered user. Other uses are maintaining a "shopping basket" of goods selected for purchase during a session at a website, website personalization (presenting different pages to different users), and tracking a particular user's visits to a website. Users who do not want their browsing and purchasing information collected can set their browser to prevent the use of cookies.

Database: A structured collection of records or information. There are a wide variety of databases, from simple tables stored in a single file to very large databases with millions of records, stored in rooms full of disk drives.

Dead Link: (*also* **Broken Link**) A URL or web address to a website that no longer exists.

Digital Image (JPEG, TIFF, GIF, PNG, etc.): A representation of a two-dimensional image as a finite set of digital values, called pixels (short for "picture elements"). Typically, the pixels are stored in computer memory as a raster image or raster map, a two-dimensional array of small integers.

These values are often transmitted or stored in a compressed form (*e.g.*, images with a document type of *.jpeg*, *.png*, or *.gif*, etc.).

Digitize: To take something that is in a non-digital format, such as an audiocassette recording or a photograph, and turn it into a digital format for distribution on computers or the Internet.

Domain Name: A name, usually words or a combination of letters and numbers, that identifies a specific website or set of websites on the Internet. For example, the domain name for **http://www.loc.gov/exhibits/gadd/4403.html** is *loc.gov* which tells you the type of organization (.gov or government in this case) as well as the organization (loc or Library of Congress).

Domain Name System (DNS): A system that stores information about host names and domain names on networks, such as the Internet. Most importantly, it provides an IP (Internet Protocol) address for each host name, and lists the mail exchange servers accepting email for each domain. The DNS forms a vital part of the Internet, because hardware requires IP addresses to perform routing, but humans use host names and domain names, for example in URLs and email addresses.

Download: To take a file that resides on a server and move it to another, usually smaller, computer via the Internet or FTP.

ejournal: A journal published on the Internet rather than in print.

email: (*short for* **Electronic Mail**) Notes, memos, and letters that can be sent from one person to another using an "email address."

email address: An electronic address in the format "username@host.domain" for sending email.

ezine: A magazine published on the Internet rather than in print.

Fair Use Doctrine: A body of law and court decisions that provides for limitations and exceptions to copyright protection in the United States. Fair use attempts to balance the interests of copyright holders with the public interest in the wider distribution and use of creative works by allowing certain limited uses that would otherwise be considered infringement of copyright.

FAQ (Frequently Asked Questions): A question-and-answer forum, usually about a particular website or its topic.

Flickr.com: A photosharing website that has become one of the largest repositories of digital photographic images in the world. Users upload hundreds of thousands of photographs each week to this Web 2.0 database.

FTP (File Transfer Protocol): A part of the Internet protocol suite that is able to transfer computer files between machines with widely different operating systems.

GIF (Graphic Interchange Format): A file format used for graphics on the Internet that allows browsers to display graphics. The *.gif* format is more appropriate for line drawings or maps because it provides more precise image definition. The *.jpg* or *.jpeg* format is preferred to the *.gif* format for color photographs because the *.gif* format allows only 256 colors.

Hit: Each occurrence of a user accessing of a website. The popularity of websites is generally measured in "hits per day." "Hits," however, are not the most accurate accounting of actual visitors to a website because "hits" records every file accessed on a page. For example, if a webpage contains text and five images, a weblog will record six hits. Logs define a "visit" as all hits made by a unique computer during a half-hour period, so this is a more accurate number, but "visits" does not differentiate between a five-second and a thirty-minute visit. A third option is to count "page views," which more accurately records the number of complete pages accessed by users.

Homepage: The webpage that serves as a starting point or table of contents for a website. It can also mean a personal website in its entirety.

Host: (*also* **Server**) A computer that holds the webpage and is connected to the Internet so that other users (called "clients") can access it.

HTML (Hypertext Markup Language): The basic code in which most webpages are written.

HTTP (Hypertext Transfer Protocol): The method in which webpages are sent from the host to the user's browser.

Hyperlink: (*also* **Link**) Text that the user can click to go to another document or part of the website.

Hypertext System: A system for displaying information that contains references (called "hyperlinks") to other information on the system, and for easily publishing, updating, and searching for the information. The most well-known hypertext system is the World Wide Web.

Icon: A graphic symbol on which the user can click to go to another document or part of the website.

Instant Messenger (IM): A computer application that allows instant text communication between two or more people through a network such as the Internet. Instant messaging differs from email in that conversations happen in real time. Common IM interfaces include Yahoo! Messenger, IRC, AIM, and Windows Messenger.

Internet: A worldwide network of networks in which computers ("clients") communicate with servers ("hosts") or other computers using a variety of methods and for a variety of purposes, including accessing pages on the World Wide Web (WWW) or email.

IP (Internet Protocol) Address: A unique number used by computers to refer to each other when sending information through the Internet. This allows machines passing the information onward on behalf of the sender to know where to send it next. Converting to these numbers from the more human-readable form of domain addresses, such as "www.example.com," is done via the Domain Name System. The process of conversion is known as resolution of domain names.

Java: A computer language used widely on the Internet to make more sophisticated applications capable of producing animations, calculations, or database functions.

JPEG (Joint Photographic Experts Group): A file format that allows browsers to display graphics. The *.jpg* or *.jpeg* format is preferred to the *.gif* format for color photographs because the *.gif* format allows only 256 colors. The *.gif* format is more appropriate for line drawings or maps because it provides more precise image definition.

Keyword: Used in Internet searching, any word or set of words that is likely to appear on a website or that sums up part or all of the content of a particular website.

Link: *See* **Hyperlink.**

Listserv: An email discussion group or its mailing list.

Login: As a verb, to access a website using a login name and a password (sometimes called "logging on"). As a noun, the pseudonym used to access a website.

Mailing List: An electronic mailing list by which an electronic newsletter or website updates are sent to the email addresses of many individuals.

Malware: A type of software used by hackers to intrude on your computer without your consent, allowing them access to your stored data (including passwords) and possibly to seize control of your computer for their own purposes.

Metadata: Data about data. A good example is a library catalog card that contains data about the nature and location of a book — it is data about the information in the book. Metadata has become important on the World Wide Web because of the need to find useful information from the mass of information available.

Mirror: Websites that are exact replicas of the original website, but hosted elsewhere to prevent congestion or too many hits on one website at one time.

Modem: A device used by a computer to turn digital signals into analog signals to be sent over a phone line to another computer.

MP3: Based on MPEG technology, this is a file format for high-quality audio.

MPEG (Motion Picture Experts Group): A standard format for audio and video files frequently found on the Internet.

Netiquette: Proper and appropriate behavior on the Internet.

Netizen: An involved member of the Internet community, such as someone who has a blog or regularly posts (writes and publishes) opinions on websites.

Newsgroup: An electronic forum for discussing a particular topic where queries and responses are posted to a website.

Online: Originally meaning that someone was logged in to a particular service and thus "online," it now describes anything that resides on the Internet.

Password: A personal code used to access a computer account.

PDF (Portable Document Format): A common format for sharing formatted documents over the Internet. Users need the free Adobe Acrobat software in order to view the document.

Podcast: An audio or video recording that is converted into an *.mp3* file so that it can be downloaded and played on portable audio or video devices such as Apple's popular iPod.

Posting: A comment or article written by a user on a blog website or newsgroup.

Public Domain: The body of creative works and other knowledge — writing, artwork, music, science, inventions, and others — in which no person or organization has any proprietary interest. Such works and inventions are considered part of the public's cultural heritage, and anyone can use and build upon them without restriction.

QTVR (QuickTime Virtual Reality): A format for viewing a three-dimensional or panoramic view.

Search Engine: A function of a website that allows you to search for items on that website. Some websites, such as Altavista and Google, are search engines for many websites.

Server: A computer software application that carries out some task on behalf of users. This is usually divided into file serving, allowing users to store and access files on a common computer, and application serving, where the software runs a computer program to carry out some task for the users. The term is now also used to mean the physical computer on which the software runs.

Social Networking Websites: Websites designed to allow ways for users to interact through chatting; blogging; sharing files, images, or video; or joining discussion groups. On popular social networking sites such as MySpace, Facebook, and Bebo, users create a profile and invite "friends" to view their profiles and interact. Some sites allow users to create groups based on shared interests and to discuss common topics.

Spider: A computer program that maps or finds all the webpages at a certain website.

Subscription Website: A website that requires a monthly or annual contribution in order to access its content.

Streaming Media: Audio or video that "streams" continuously through a player such as Real Audio or Windows Media Player instead of first requiring a download.

TCP/IP (Transmission Control Protocol/Internet Protocol): The group of universal formats by which computers transmit and receive data on the Internet.

Upload: To send a file from one, usually smaller, computer to a server or host.

URL (Uniform Resource Locator): The "address" or "location" of a website. URLs are in the form "hostname.domain," for example, **bedfordstmartins.com**, and usually preceded by *http://*.

Username: (*also* **Login Name**) A pseudonym used to login (or log on) to a website. (*See* **Login**.)

Vlog (Video Blog): A blog that is created as a video file rather than a text.

Web 2.0: Refers to second-generation Internet developments such as wikis and social networking websites, such as Flickr, MySpace, or Facebook.

Web Browser: (*also* **Browser**) A software package that enables a user to display and interact with HTML documents hosted by web servers. The largest networked collection of hypertext documents is known as the World Wide Web. Common web browsers include Internet Explorer, Netscape Navigator, Safari, and Firefox.

Weblog: *See* **Blog**.

Website: A virtual place on the World Wide Web that contains multimedia and text. Websites all have a URL that "web browsers" can use to locate them.

Wiki: Refers to software platforms that allow users to create and edit content on a website. The most popular wiki-based website is the online encyclopedia *Wikipedia:* **http://en.wikipedia.org/wiki/Main_Page**.

WWW (World Wide Web): A medium on the Internet used for multimedia and interactive electronic communication using "web browsers" such as Internet Explorer, Opera, or Netscape.

YouTube.com: A Web 2.0 community that is built around the sharing of video content. YouTube.com users upload hundreds of thousands of video files each week.

Alphabetical List of Websites Reviewed

Numbers refer to the website entry numbers, not page numbers.

Index

Types of primary sources are listed in *italics*; regions are listed in **bold**. Numbers refer to the website entry numbers, not page numbers.